FOR THE

OF PREACHING

To DONNA

WITH LOVE

Gust & Diane

FOR THE *Love* OF PREACHING

The Life Story *of* Howard F. Sugden

DON DENYES

For additional copies, contact Wellington House Publishers at
517.322.2000 or wellingtonhouse@southlife.com.

ISBN 0-9763467-0-2

Printed in the United States of America

To Howard's faithful wife,
Lucile,
Lover of God's Word, and dear friend.

And to my faithful wife,
Nancy,
Lover of God's Word, the jewel of my life,
and my best friend.

CONTENTS

FOREWORD

IF ever a man followed the apostle Paul's "this one thing I do" (Phil. 3:13), that man was Howard F. Sugden. The "one thing" that compelled and consumed him was to preach the Word of God and do it in such a way that people would hear, understand, and obey what God had to say. This was his highest calling and his greatest joy, and he did it well.

I doubt that there were many times when Howard wasn't thinking about sermons. My wife and I accompanied him and Lucile on a vacation trip to Hawaii, and while at Pearl Harbor, we saw a large freighter that had recently suffered a severe fire. "The boat has been purchased by a shipping firm," said our guide, "and they plan to restore it." Howard asked how much the firm had paid for the ship, and when he heard the huge amount, he took out his pen and a three-by-five card and made a notation. As he did, he said to me, "Isn't it amazing how much people will pay just to restore something?" He had another sermon illustration for his file.

On two occasions the four of us traveled to Great Britain for holidays, primarily to visit the churches where the great preachers had ministered, the homiletical heroes whose pictures were hanging on Howard's library walls. He was in his glory standing behind the pulpit of Free St. George's church in Edinburgh, where Alexander Whyte had ministered, and also visiting Robert Murray McCheyne's church in Dundee (we held McCheyne's Bible) and George Morrison's church in Glasgow. I could tell Howard was storing up impressions that would be woven perfectly into the fabric of future messages. He had what my old professor Dr. Lloyd Perry used to call "the homiletical mind-set," and this was one of the secrets of his ministry. He was always thinking preaching.

We often ministered together in conferences, and it was a delight to watch him as well as listen to him. You were never sure what he would do next. One of his assistants whispered to me at a service, "Pastor is a bit of a showman." Not a show-off but a real expert who knew how to use his voice, his gestures, and his rich vocabulary to capture and hold the attention of the listening congregation, including the children, teenagers, and college students, who loved him. It was difficult to be distracted when Howard was preaching.

He was a disciplined man. He arrived at the church early each morning and went to his library. (One morning he accidentally tripped the alarm system and found himself looking into the faces of several police officers.) He had a desk for each message he was preparing that week, and the books he used remained on the desks until the messages were completed. During one of our British trips, he brought along a briefcase filled with commentaries on Hebrews, just in case he had time to study.

Howard exemplified the "old-fashioned" kind of minister who worked hard to serve God and the church. He cared personally for his people and prepared nutritious spiritual meals for them week by week. He walked with God. He and Lucile were a team, and she was his strength in the area where he was weak. I think he should have listened more to her counsel, but they labored together happily and were a blessing to many. Often as they drove to meetings they would sing together or discuss some Bible truth.

Howard Sugden was unique, and some would say perhaps a bit eccentric, but you couldn't help but love him and rejoice to be his friend. When he was trying to work his way out of some problem he'd created for himself, you wanted to drop everything and help him out. Often he phoned me to discuss a church situation. He already knew what to do; he just needed somebody to encourage him to do it. When his gifted mind began to falter, we felt the pain, but he could still quote yards of Scripture, poetry, and hymnody. It was an honor to minister at his funeral. As the long motorcade made its way to the cemetery, I could imagine Howard in heaven, chatting with Spurgeon and Campbell Morgan and Billy Sunday.

I miss him, but the best is yet to come; and we may join in that conversation sooner than we expect.

Warren W. Wiersbe
Lincoln, Nebraska
October 2004

PREFACE

"People learn from one another,
just as iron sharpens iron."
—*Proverbs 27:17 The English Version*

THE kingly writer of Proverbs had a point. It is God's plan to improve our lives through the lives of others. When we humans come in close contact with each other, we can anticipate experiencing the exciting process of transformation.

The whole process can easily have the reverse effect. If we grind our life against a marred individual, with the nasty burrs of bad character, we will not be helped. Some people will improve you. Others will damage you. Like sandpaper on glass, they scratch the surface of your life and dull your finish. Yet we must not let this potential danger hinder us from the benefit of spiritual development through personal relationships. Simply put, we must choose wisely those individuals we allow to sharpen and shape us.

King David probably taught this principle of iron sharpening iron to his son Solomon. He also, no doubt, instructed his son on selecting proper companions, friends who would give him an edge. David said, "I am a friend to all who fear you, to all who obey your word" (Psalm 119:63). That's the secret! Make godly friends your file if you want to be fashioned into a person who fears God.

13

"But how can I connect with a godly person who is geographically distant, or walk with the saints of past generations?" someone might say. The answer, biography! The lives of great men and women of God who are removed from us can still sharpen us as we read about their journeys and make them our companions.

One such servant of God, whose life is fine steel, is Dr. Howard Frederic Sugden (1907–1993). Though he was relatively unknown, Howard's dedication to God during more than sixty years of ministry in two countries and four churches is an encouraging story.

Extremely tenderhearted toward people, yet driven in his work, Howard was servant to a single passion that dominated his life—he loved to preach God's Word.

Pastors will be sharpened as they walk with this "pastor of pastors." During the height of his ministry, rarely a week would go by without some struggling shepherd traveling a great distance to spend time with this seasoned servant. He would patiently and unselfishly share his knowledge with them as he opened his heart to their concerns. Howard Sugden spent much of his time traveling throughout North America holding extended meetings in churches and Bible conferences. Nothing thrilled him more than preaching God's Word and encouraging God's people.

Along the way, he developed and maintained a wonderful David and Jonathan relationship with Dr. Warren Wiersbe, in spite of a wide difference in age. They were brothers in the faith, incurable lovers of good books, and kindred spirits in their passion for preaching. Often the great bookstores of Grand Rapids, Michigan would contain the easy banter and loud laughter of these two servants of God as they would walk up and down the aisles, commenting about books and assessing their value. Dr. Wiersbe calls Sugden "a gifted expositor and loving pastor with a winsome sense of humor . . . [and] the ability to make the Scriptures come alive to the contemporary mind." Iron sharpening iron!

If you are a believer in Jesus Christ, this story will challenge your spiritual life as you learn of Dr. Sugden's pure and simple devotion to the Savior. If you are involved in the preaching ministry, your love for that magnificent calling will be increased and your commitment to the task enhanced. In short, your life will be sharpened by Howard's steel! So, let the filing begin!

ACKNOWLEDGEMENTS

I wish to acknowledge the invaluable assistance of Lucile Sugden who, at the age of 94 (she is now 97), gave me wonderful insight into her life with Howard. This biography, written with her approval, could not have been written without her generous contribution.

A special thanks to Warren Wiersbe for his keen observations of Howard's life and ministry. I am grateful for his willingness to spend long hours on the phone sharing his memories amidst hearty laughter and tears. Dr. Wiersbe was not only a significant source of information, he remains a constant source of inspiration.

I am indebted to my executive assistant, Marilyn Oldham, and her husband, John. Long were the hours they poured into this project from its inception. Such devotion cannot be forgotten. Also, to the entire support staff at South—Laura Bevan, Sandy Rinck, and Nancy Bassett—thank you for your patience and assistance.

I also wish to acknowledge Haddon Robinson for his wise counsel and oversight of this work, although he should not be held accountable for its imperfections. Dr. Robinson continues to model to preachers everywhere what it means to clearly communicate God's truth.

Thank you also to Julie Ackerman Link for her wonderful work preparing the text for printing, and to Bev Cassel for her artistic skills in designing the cover.

Jim Hunsucker, Kevin Shaw, Bev Wallace, and Sheila Rynbrandt were skillful editors of the manuscript and deserve high praise for their counsel.

Gratitude also to those who gave valuable insight into Howard's life through personal interviews, e-mail, and letters. Many of those helpful contributors are mentioned in the endnotes.

I would like to express my appreciation to the people of South Church for giving me the freedom and encouragement to pursue this project. You enjoyed Howard for forty years and have endured me for ten, because you love the truth. It is a joy to serve Christ with you.

Finally, I am forever grateful to my family for their unconditional love. I wish to thank my wife, Nancy, and our five daughters—Kari, Kristin, Kimberly, Katie, and Kendra—for always supporting me with their encouragement and patience. No husband or father could be more proud.

INTRODUCTION

HE could not quit. This had been his whole life. For over sixty years he had given his time and energy to this demanding work and the thought of stepping down was more than he could bear. Tears filled his eyes. A strange mixture of satisfaction and sorrow filled his soul. But it was time. The evident signs of a weakened warrior could not be denied: the halting step, the failing memory, the repetition of the same illustration in the same sermon. Both his speech and his balance were proving unsteady. It was time to step down.

On this last day of the decade, December 31, 1989, Howard Sugden was retiring as pastor of the South Baptist Church in Lansing, Michigan, a post he held for over thirty-five years. More importantly, it was the end of a lifetime of pastoral work that spanned a large section of the twentieth century, over six decades of giving himself to the love of his life—preaching the gospel of Jesus Christ.

How can any individual be completely focused on a task as challenging as preaching? What kept him going? What shaped him into a man consumed with communicating the gospel of Christ? Where did he get his passion and strength to endure so much for so many years? It all started in a small rural town located in the thumb region of Lower Michigan.

CHAPTER 1

THE MAN FROM MAYVILLE

I grew up in a home where many problems were settled
around the kitchen table in prayer.
—*Howard F. Sugden*

AFTER prolonged dickering with the wealthy gentleman, the deal was finally done. Charles Thomas Sugden now owned 240 acres of beautiful ground just north of the picturesque town of Mayville. The year was 1918. Although partially wooded, 200 acres could easily be cleared (if clearing land is ever easy) and used to establish a workable farm. Indians happened to live in the woods adjacent to the new Sugden farm, and through the years they would prove to be congenial neighbors. A farm: not a bad idea when you have three boys to raise, and the Lord knows that a fourth is on the way!

Charles, born in 1881, had moved with his family of eight siblings from England, settling in Michigan. Shortly thereafter, this energetic young Englishman met a beautiful German girl and quickly fell in love. Ida May Lichtenfedt had come from a broken home and experienced a very difficult childhood. At an early age she was separated from her mother and spent most of her life living with her father. Years later Howard would say, "My grandfather was the finest old gentleman I ever met . . . when he was sober. Otherwise, he was a disaster."[1]

Consequently, Ida's young life had been filled with sorrow. When, at the age of nineteen, she received a proposal from Charles, she gladly accepted, and they were married at the turn of a new century, in 1903.

After a brief move to California, where Charles worked with relatives as a muleskinner taking supplies to the oil fields, the young couple was convinced that a better life could be found back in the Midwest. They decided to return to Michigan and start a family. The Sugdens were ultimately blessed with five children; Ora, called Orie (1904); Howard (1907); Thelma, who died immediately after birth (1909); Duane, also known as Dewey (1913); and Elmer (1921). For a family with four boys, the farm would be the ideal place to live.

The Sugdens welcomed their second son into the world on April 4, 1907, in Kingston, Michigan, and named him Howard Frederic. He was named after president Howard Taft, with his middle name taken from his maternal grandfather. He was only eleven years old when his family moved to the 240 acres in Mayville.

Outside of his family, the farm quickly became the most powerful influence in shaping his early character. Like most other farms around the time of World War I, the Sugden estate was a humble place with plenty of work to do. The land always needed clearing from roots and rocks so the crops, mainly potatoes, could be planted.

Then there were the endless chores of caring for animals (chickens, cows, horses, pigs, and black angus cattle), all clamoring for special attention. Since Elmer wasn't born until the early twenties, and Dewey was still a small boy of five, most of the chores fell to Orie and Howard.

A CLOSE KNIT COMMUNITY

If the farm was a wonderful place to raise a family, Mayville was the perfect place to experience community. The population was approximately 750, and the kids knew they were cared for by all of them. Everyone knew everyone, which made it almost impossible to misbehave without parental knowledge. On Saturday nights most families would congregate in town. The men would get a shave, the women would trade eggs for dry goods, and the children would play together for hours. The community was extremely close.

Charles Sugden was known throughout the district for his honest character, warm personality, and his keen interest in people. The Sugdens were addicted to hospitality. They regularly had guests over for dinner or evening conversation. Ida, who loved to cook and bake, was always making something for someone. If the little brown house wasn't filled with company, the family would often play games (except for playing cards—they were strictly forbidden). Other nights would find them in the large living room, gathered around the old Victrola or the upright piano, singing the night away![2] Charles loved to sing and passed that love on to his second son. The Sugdens might have been living on the edge of poverty, but they were rich in love.

However, Charles could also be a demanding father and a strict disciplinarian. He was, as everyone could observe, a serious man of the times. He would often quote to his boys a familiar line from Alexander Pope, "Order is heaven's first law."[3] He made sure that everything on the farm followed his orders. Charles and Ida loved the boys in their own quiet way, but any open display of affection was as rare as a free day from farm work. Once, when Howard was eager to ignore his chores so he could play with his friends, his father laid down the law. "First you cultivate the corn, then you can play." Howard rushed through his work and hurried off to be with his buddies, leaving behind him many crooked rows in the field. When his father discovered the irregular rows, he went searching for Howard, brought him back to the field, and made him plow the entire field again, this time with straight and orderly rows![4]

THE POPULAR ONE

Howard was full of energy and always on the go. He never walked into the house, he flew into it.[5] This trait was clearly derived from his mother, who was described as "107 pounds of true lightning."[6] Perhaps it was this same boundless energy that gave him aspirations of becoming a boxer. It certainly wasn't his size! Being rather short and slim in build, he could barely make bantam-weight, but he enjoyed boxing while in high school and did quite well from his own accounts.

In reality, he was not a fighter but a lover. He loved people and people loved him. When he would walk the few miles from the farm into town, kids would follow him in *pied piper* fashion. "I think the people loved him because he made them feel so good. He always treated them like they were very important!" his younger brother, Elmer, remembered.[7]

Howard was quite optimistic and carefree. God had blessed him with a wonderful sense of humor. "He was sort of crazy, very funny. He did not work his way through high school, *he fooled his way through*," his future wife recalled.[8] His constant joking and exceptional sense of humor led many in his immediate family to believe that he would make his living on the stage as an entertainer, not as a boxer in the ring. His natural theatrical flair would later become one of the most outstanding characteristics of his long pulpit ministry. There was no doubt that the most mischievous, dramatic, and fun loving of the Sugden boys was Howard.

There was one thing that he knew for certain, he did not want to be a farmer! He was not averse to hard work, just farm work. "I'm not very good at it," he would later confess. "I was so bad at milking, even the cows got nervous when I came into the barn!"[9] But hard work strengthens the soul as well as the body, and the work of the farm developed Howard in both areas.

CONVERSION

The family attended a small Lutheran church for a time, then moved their membership to the Mills Memorial Baptist Church in the center of town. Early spiritual impressions were difficult to detect in Howard's carefree life, until a crisis brought him face to face with death. While in high school, he became extremely ill. He was rushed to nearby Saginaw where the doctor diagnosed the problem as an acute ruptured appendix. The physicians felt that the peritonitis was too far advanced to save him. Charles and Ida talked freely with the doctor in Howard's presence about the grim prospect of his condition. They feared he would not live through the night. One doctor curtly told the family, "You can leave him here tonight and come back to pick up his body in the morning."[10] When the room finally cleared of callers and he was left alone, Howard cried out to God for help. He made a deal with God reminiscent of Jacob's proposition in Genesis 28. Howard prayed, "God, if you will pull me through,

I'll give my life to you!" God did graciously spare his life, but Howard somehow forgot his end of the bargain. Although he had grown up in a Christian home, he was not yet a Christian. He was more conscious of God now, to be sure, but not yet a child of God.

Whenever he could get away from the daily chores of the farm, Howard loved to hunt. In March of 1926, one hunting trip proved to be anything but enjoyable. The eighteen-year-old Howard was in the woods just north of his home with a very close friend. Howard's gun accidentally went off, narrowly missing his companion. For a moment he feared he had actually killed him. How relieved he was to discover that the bullet had harmlessly disappeared in the woods. But this ordeal, a second encounter with death, left him deeply shaken. He turned to his friend and said, "We need to find God and set this right!" They ended their hunting trip prematurely and immediately headed home.[11]

Upon returning to Mayville, the boys discovered that special meetings were being held in town at Mills Memorial. Evangelist P. H. Kadey from Flint was conducting a four-week evangelistic campaign. Having found a new interest in eternal things, the boys determined to go to the meeting that night. The Holy Spirit, who had been pursuing Howard for some time, intensified His efforts. Through the clear preaching of the Gospel of Christ, the Spirit brought conviction to Howard's soul and drew him to Jesus. When an invitation was given to trust Christ, Howard, along with two of his buddies, gladly prayed to trust Jesus as his Savior.[12]

He never forgot what happened on that day! Only three weeks shy of his nineteenth birthday, Howard Sugden became a child of God! A four-by-six card found in one of the last Bibles Howard would ever own simply told the story.

Howard wrote this card in his later years and inadvertently made a mistake on the date; he was born in 1907.

The change was immediate. He began reading the Bible whenever he could extract a few free minutes from his daily chores. For instance, while plowing a field with the three-horse team, he would finish a furrow, then he would sit down to read his New Testament. After a few minutes he would get up, plow another furrow, and sit down once more to read the Word. When his father questioned this unusual practice, Howard replied, "The horses need a rest!"[13] This creative plowing strategy likely owed more to a hungry soul rather than to the tired horses. He simply could not get enough of God's Word.

H. H. SAVAGE

This insatiable love for the Scriptures was further encouraged by the pioneer radio ministry of Dr. Henry H. Savage. Dr. Savage had been pastoring the First Baptist Church of Pontiac, Michigan, since 1924. On March 2, 1926, the same month in which Howard was converted to Christ, Dr. Savage started one of the very first religious broadcasts involving a Sunday morning church service over Detroit's WJR radio. Savage was an influential leader and one of the most beloved Bible teachers in the state. Each Sunday Howard would finish his chores in time to sit by the Atwater Kent radio and listen to "The Sunday School of the Air," with the forceful preaching of this respected man of God.[14]

The Bible was taught with such clarity and power that Howard not only had his soul fed, but his heart was surprisingly stirred. Suddenly Howard developed a growing passion to preach this Word of God. "Could God be calling me to proclaim His Word?" That was the constant question tugging on his heart.

Upon reflection, one can clearly see that the preaching style of Savage did much to shape the future preaching of Sugden. There was clear Bible teaching from a dispensational perspective with unquestioning confidence in the authority and reliability of the Scriptures. The lives of these two men would intersect many times throughout the coming years.

On the flyleaf of one of Howard's Bibles, he had penned these words. "When God makes the prophet, He does not unmake the man."[15] God took a happy-go-lucky, hard working farm boy who wasn't too keen on schooling or the farm, but who had an honest love for people and a boundless passion for life and laughter, and made him passionate for Christ and His Word.

He was still rough around the edges, and if he was going to preach, he needed help. Although his local church was a means of encouragement, and the radio ministry of Savage spiritually enriching, he desired more training than these could offer. Upon reaching this conclusion, Howard decided to attend Moody Bible Institute, the place where Henry Savage received his training. If it was good enough for Savage, it would be good enough for him. Against the wishes of his father, who longed for his son to be a farmer, Howard set out for Chicago to prepare for the gospel ministry. The popular boy from Mayville was planning to preach. But it wasn't going to be that easy.

MOODY BIBLE INSTITUTE

In the spring of 1927, Howard attended Moody Bible Institute to deepen his knowledge of the Word of God. His stay proved to be surprisingly brief. He attended during the months of March and April, but abruptly departed for home without finishing any course or program.[16] What went wrong? Two factors precipitated the move back to Michigan. First, there was the difficulty of the scholastic studies at Moody. Adjusting to the rigors of a college education, with a poor high school track record, was a daunting task. But the stronger force came from his father. Charles continued to urge Howard to return to the farm, and Howard found his father's voice convincing.

In later years Howard would return to Moody, not as a student, but as a highly regarded speaker at Founders Week. The school always held a place in his heart. The feeling must have been mutual because in 1986 he was made an honorary alumnus of Moody.[17]

But now he was back home, reluctantly working on the family farm. And while he still held to the hope of becoming a preacher of the Gospel, such a dream was at risk of being lost forever. Who could tell which path would prevail, the plowman or the preacher?

END NOTES

1. Howard Sugden. *What a Life!* A sermon delivered at South Baptist Church, Lansing, Michigan; March 12, 1989.

2. Personal interview with Elmer and Pauline Sugden and Diane Smith, August 19, 2002.

3. Howard Sugden. *What a Life!* A sermon delivered at South Baptist Church, Lansing, Michigan; March 12, 1989.

4. Personal interview with Elmer and Pauline Sugden, August 2002.

5. Personal interview with Diane Smith, August 2002.

6. Howard Sugden. *What a Life!* A sermon delivered at South Baptist Church, Lansing, Michigan; March 12, 1989.

7. Personal interview with Elmer and Pauline Sugden, August 2002.

8. Personal interview with Lucile Sugden, June 2001.

9. Personal interview with Lucile Sugden, October 2002.

10. Ibid.

11. Personal interview with Lucile Sugden, June 2001.

12. Ibid.

13. Ibid.

14. *Gospel Echoes.* Published by First Baptist Church, Pontiac, Michigan; December 1961.

15. Dr. Sam Hoyt. *Dedication of the Howard Sugden Chapel.* A sermon delivered at South Baptist Church, Lansing, Michigan; April 1994.

16. Millie Brown. Alumni Association, Moody Bible Institute; September 2002.

17. *Lansing State Journal.* Lansing, Michigan; October 15, 1986.

CHAPTER 2

PARTNERS FOR LIFE

The smartest thing I ever did was
to marry her. —Howard F. Sugden

IT was the fall of 1927 when a young blonde arrived in Mayville to teach the commercial courses at the local high school. In addition to the normal business subjects of bookkeeping and typing, she would introduce a brand new course to the curriculum, shorthand. Lucile Miller was born May 31, 1907, on a farm four miles north of Angola, Indiana. At the age of ten she moved with her sizable family to establish a permanent homestead on a tract of land near the quaint town of Reading, in a southern area of Lower Michigan.

Lucile was the very middle child of thirteen, having three older and three younger sets of brothers and sisters. Her mother was a strong woman who managed her family like a general, issuing the orders and assigning the chores for her brood.[1] Such a determined and strong willed woman apparently passed her genes on to her diminutive seventh child. Lucile was a young woman with great strength of character and incredible determination.

She attended a tiny one-room country schoolhouse containing eight grades and only one instructor. From the fourth grade on, she had a Christian teacher who had a profound impact on all her students. Miss Vina Terpening was one of those unique individuals who lovingly planted the seed of God's truth into the hearts of her students by her words and her example. It is rare to find this harmony between one's pronouncements and one's practice. The impression of a life well lived gives context, substance, and power to the spoken word. The converse is also true. Benjamin Franklin used to say:

> A life full of words but containing no deeds, is like a life full of weeds. For when the weeds began to grow, the mouth doth overflow![2]

Miss Terpening not only piqued Lucile's interest in spiritual matters, she also created in her a passion for the teaching profession. "I wanted to become just like her, so I worked very hard to become a teacher," Lucile affirmed many years later.[3] As a result, Lucile was dedicated to becoming a teacher, and she never wavered from that course.

Showing both her independent mind and her growing spiritual interest, Lucile decided one night that she would attend a special meeting at a local church, even though no one else in the family was inclined to go. She hitched up the horses to the wagon by herself, and traveled the several miles to the small Methodist Church in town. That night the Lord revealed Himself to Lucile, and she received Christ as her Savior. She had been very curious about God, but uncommitted. Now she clearly understood the good news of the gospel, and embraced Christ wholeheartedly. The seed that Vina Terpening had been sowing in her classroom with a small group of students was now bearing eternal fruit.

MEETING IN MAYVILLE

Upon completing high school, Lucile studied at the Teachers College in Ypsilanti (now Eastern Michigan University), receiving a degree in business in 1927. Two promising teaching opportunities were immediately presented to her. She weighed the benefits of each and chose the position at Mayville High. Little did she realize what a significant impact this seemingly insignificant choice would make on her life! God was at work behind the scenes, directing Lucile to the proper location. Lines from the pen of William Cowper, words that Howard would often recite in future ministry, seemed so pertinent to Lucile's situation:

> *God moves in a mysterious way*
> *His wonders to perform;*
> *He plants His footsteps on the seas,*
> *And rides upon the storm.*

In the late summer of 1927, Lucile made the move to Mayville. After securing a room from Jane Johnston, an older lady in town, and locating a church to attend on Sunday mornings, she finally settled down into the small town.

On that first Sunday, she visited the Mills Memorial Baptist Church, and the first person to welcome her was a greeter by the name of Charles Sugden. Howard's father had a warm personality and a great love for people, which made him an outstanding greeter. Sunday after Sunday he welcomed every person who walked through the front doors of the church.

After the morning service, he went home and told Howard, "I met the new little school teacher that came to town, and I really think you should meet her!"[4] Apparently Howard did not follow his father's advice immediately. Orie got the first date with Miss Miller. However, Howard soon joined in the competition for her attention. The two got acquainted on a youth choir trip to the city of Lapeer. Howard asked Lucile out for a date. The match was an instant success! Lucile's interest quickly shifted from the older to the younger brother. While Orie was upset for a time, he eventually got over it. Howard, however, was hooked!

PROPOSAL

Over the next year, their dates revolved around church activities in Mayville. Howard did some occasional teaching in the church, and in spite of his youth, was elected to the official board of the church at the age of nineteen.[5] Lucile played the piano for some church services and many youth meetings. Much of their free time together was invested in serving the Lord. Both were sensing that God had purposefully brought them together. And now it was time to get serious.

On a fall night in 1928, while riding in the back seat of a car on a double date with Orie and his girl, Howard leaned over to Lucile and asked for her hand in marriage. Without hesitation she accepted. But when Howard talked about going to Lucile's home that Christmas, her response shocked him. "I'm not taking you home with me unless we are married," she insisted. "The sooner the better," Howard thought. He agreed without hesitation!

On December 21, 1928, Lucile taught a full day of classes at the high school, finishing at four o'clock. She quickly left school to meet Howard and together they drove the twenty-plus miles south to Lapeer, to be married at five o'clock in the home of their former Mayville pastor, Rev. Henry Zimmer. They commandeered Irene Travis and Andrew Cherpes, two teachers from the high school, to serve as bridesmaid and best man respectively. Howard's immediate family made up the rest of the congregation. Within thirty minutes, Howard Frederic Sugden and Marguerite Lucile Miller were husband and wife. This marriage would form a partnership that would last almost sixty-five years, and accomplished what any marriage should accomplish, making two people far better together than they could ever be on their own. After they had been married for over fifty-eight years, Howard confided to a local newspaper reporter, "The smartest thing I ever did was to marry her." They were indeed true partners for life!

CALL TO MINISTRY

After a brief honeymoon, the newlyweds were back in Mayville living with Howard's parents. The battle in Howard's heart between the plow and the pulpit raged on, but the pulpit clearly had the edge! The teaching of Henry Savage continued to propel Howard toward a preaching vocation. His first sermon, which was delivered at the remote Forest Lawn Methodist Protestant Church near Mayville, was a positive experience. He possessed a growing, deep internal conviction that God was calling him to preach.

But Howard did not want to disappoint his father. Charles had purchased another farm in the area and planned to have his son take it over after his marriage to Lucile. The struggle was intense, not because he loved farming, but because he loved his father. Nevertheless, a new passion had now consumed his soul.

Like Jeremiah, he could honestly say, "His word was in my heart like a burning fire shut up in my bones; I was weary of holding it back, and I could not" (Jeremiah 20:9).

"I just have to preach the gospel," he confided to Lucile. Her response was as simple as it was wise. "All right then, if you are going to go into the ministry, then you are going to college to be trained."[6]

Relieved when the decision was made, Howard then broke the news to his father. Charles could see that it was futile to fight any longer. Howard's farming days were over. Although he left farming, he never forgot the farm. Throughout his life he would recall his rural roots and the important lessons he learned during those difficult days. In the years ahead he would often praise the Lord for his early days on the farm.

The path before Howard and Lucile now was clear—ministerial training. Direction they had, but what about a destination? Moody Bible Institute in Chicago was the most obvious choice. Howard had enjoyed his time there and was in agreement with their doctrinal focus. Moody had a wonderful heritage, a fine reputation, and excellent faculty. But how could the young couple afford to live in that expensive city?

GO SOUTH!

It was Lucile's older brother, Roy, who told the newlyweds about a unique college in Kimberly Heights, Tennessee, near Knoxville. The genius of Johnson Bible College was found in its practical mission to prepare men for the ministry. The college, which began in January 1886 as a correspondence Bible school, opened it doors as *The School of the Evangelists* in 1893. It "was born in the heart of Ashley S. Johnson, who had a vision of a

36

place where poor young men could come, work, and study to become ministers of the gospel of Christ."[7] Realizing that many pastors in that day had not completed their high school education, JBC provided, along with its college training, an academy for that purpose.

Lucile discovered that she could teach in the academy and earn a meager income while Howard took classes in the college. The young couple, delighted with this pragmatic arrangement that seemed divinely suited for them, decided to attend Johnson. In September of 1929, Howard and Lucile piled their earthly belongings into the back of a second-hand Chevy and headed south toward the Great Smoky Mountains.

Howard had seldom been out of Michigan and the experience of a new culture was both thrilling and daunting. One can imagine the hectic pace that he and his new bride soon encountered as they entered the college scene. JBC, comprising about 115 students from approximately twenty states and Canada, was a rugged school with few amenities.[8]

Lucile was teaching the familiar commercial courses she had taught back in Mayville. She encountered few discipline problems, now that her students were all "pastors in preparation." Years later she acknowledged that the two years teaching in Tennessee were the best years of her teaching career.[9]

To further her own education, she took several courses in the college. She excelled in Greek, a subject she enjoyed due to her love for languages and the Latin background she received in high school. She even found the time to play some basketball for the college team. Lucile's value did not lie in her height. At barely five feet tall, she towered over no one. But what she lacked in height, she made up in enthusiasm, and for this they made her captain. Howard also found time for sports. He chauffeured the men's basketball team to many of its away games! Life was very full.

TWO CHALLENGES

Life at Johnson was not without its complications. Two significant challenges confronted Howard shortly after his arrival in Knoxville that fall of 1929. The first related to the feeling of unrest that existed among the student body. In 1927, Alva Ross Brown had become the new president of Johnson Bible College, and the first president to follow its founder.[10] The intelligent Pennsylvanian was a graduate of JBC and had done some work on his Masters degree at the University of Michigan in Ann Arbor. The problem was this: Alva Brown was only twenty-one years old! He was not only the youngest college president in the entire country, he was only one year older than Howard! The trustees had tried to dissuade the young Brown from taking the presidency, but he was determined to fulfill the wishes of the late president, Ashley Johnson, who had personally chosen him as his successor.

Alva's extreme youth and inexperience caused many of the students to revolt. They became belligerent and uncooperative, holding several student-led protest meetings. They refused to cooperate with the new president. Support from the friends and alumni of the school dwindled. The stock market crash of October, and the subsequent great depression which consumed the country, added to the tension on campus. The school's debts mounted.[11] Things seemed to be spiraling out of control. President Brown, who had just married in the spring of 1929, needed some moral support to face the awesome task of directing the school in the face of opposition. It would be no small blessing from God for this novice president and his new bride to find solace and sincere encouragement from another couple of newlyweds. "A friend loves at all times and a brother is born for adversity" (Proverbs 17:17). In the Sugdens, the young president found two excellent friends to support him and help him face the daunting task. Alva Ross Brown eventually survived the heat of his early administration and served Johnson Bible College until he suffered a heart attack and died in the summer of 1940. Howard and Lucile went against the tide of their peers and campus opinion to help a brother in need. Throughout their ministry, the Sugdens would become famous for their encouragement to the Lord's servants.

The second challenge Howard faced was academic. While Lucile had exchanged her Mayville students for her Knoxville scholars, she learned that her most important student was Howard. He had clowned his way through high school, struggled for two months at Moody, and now he found his studies at Johnson incredibly taxing. Howard was not unintelligent, but he was unfamiliar and untrained in some of the educational basics. Lucile, his chosen helpmate, was the one who could complete him, and she tutored him in his classes. Howard's public speaking and grammar were in particular need of attention. Greek was difficult for him to decipher. Patiently Lucile labored with her husband's educational deficiencies and his academic progress was unmistakable.

THE WORLD OF BOOKS

That fall, to help earn some income, Howard took a job in the Irwin College Library. The campus was rugged, but the library was excellent. God used this job to help Howard better combat his two major obstacles. The library became a quiet place to escape from the campus unrest, a safe haven in the student storm. He learned the benefits of getting *lost* in the library. The library work also proved advantageous in improving his intellectual skills. He became immersed in books. God created an environment to develop a passion that would last a lifetime—a fervent love for reading. He now reveled in the study he had earlier dismissed. He became familiar with the Dewey Decimal System (which he later adapted and used in his own huge library of 15,000 volumes) and captivated with the world of the printed page. Howard could heartily agree with Oswald Chambers:

"My books! I cannot tell you what they are to me—silent, wealthy, loyal lovers. To look at them, to handle them, and to reread them! I do thank God for my books with every fiber of my being. Friends that are ever true and ever your own. Why, I could have almost cried for excess of joy when I got hold of them again. I know them, I wish you could see how they look at me, a quiet calm look of certain acquaintance."[12]

Johnson Bible College was part of the Christian Church denomination. Some of its theological positions differed from what Howard had been taught as a Baptist. Being challenged in the classroom with theological positions not his own proved to be extremely beneficial. Howard was driven to examine the Scriptures for the resolutions he sought to these confusing issues. Like the Bereans of old, in Acts 17:11, he "searched the Scriptures daily to see whether these things were so." Ultimately, this doctrinal dilemma made him stronger. He became grounded in his faith, and his affinity for and acquaintance with the Holy Scriptures intensified. Like gold in the fire, Howard was refined by the trials he endured.

During this first year at Johnson, both Howard and Lucile deepened in their walk with God and their love for each other. When the pressures of life and study mounted and he needed a quiet place of refuge, Howard could often be found in the campus prayer tower. With its wonderful view of the Smoky Mountains, the tower was a spot where he could quietly enjoy the majesty of God's creation. Alone with God, he would once again remember that his strength came from the Creator of those hills, and in that strength, he could do all that God called him to do! JBC was to Howard what the backside of the desert was to Paul. It was a solitary place of retreat from the harsh demands of life where he learned to spend time alone with God, and to prepare for the battle ahead.

But where would he serve? Was there a place of service for him in God's work?

END NOTES

1. Personal interview with Lucile Sugden, June 2001.
2. Benjamin Franklin. *The Works of Benjamin Franklin*. Volume III, 1757–1775, London. In a letter to his sister dated September 16, 1758, Franklin quoted these lines and attributed them to "an Ancient Poet whose words we have all studied and copied at school."
3. Personal interview with Lucile Sugden, June 2001.
4. Ibid.
5. *Mayville Journal*. Mayville, Michigan; December 1928.
6. Personal interview with Lucile Sugden, June 2001.
7. Johnson Bible College Web site, (jbc.edu) historical section.

8. The actual registration for the year 1932–1933, the Sugdens last year at Johnson, was 118 students from 23 states & Canada. Information provided by Linda Reid of Johnson Bible College, October 2002.

9. Personal interview with Lucile Sugden, November 2002.

10. Ashley Johnson's wife, Emma, served as president the two years between her husband's death and the presidency of Alva Brown.

11. Johnson Bible College Web site (jbc.edu) historical section.

12. D. W. Lambert. Oswald Chambers, *An Unbribed Soul*. Fort Washington: Christian Literature Crusade; 1968, p. 50.

CHAPTER 3

YOU HAVE TO START SOMEWHERE!

*We are going to work. We are going to call on every house in
the neighborhood. Then we are going to call on every house
in town. Then we are going to call on every house on every
farm. We are going to work!* —Howard F. Sugden

BEFORE the Sugdens finished their first year at Johnson, they
contacted the Baptist Convention in Michigan to see if there
was any church opening for an aspiring pastor to gain some
ministerial experience. The convention told them about a
church in Perry, Michigan.

To say that the Perry Church was looking for a pastor would
be a stretch. Actually, the church had been closed for almost a
year and the situation appeared beyond hope. On January 23,
1930, the *Perry Journal* captured their desperate circumstance:

> An important business meeting of the Baptist Church of
> Perry will be held in the Church on Monday, February
> 3rd at 2 o'clock p.m. The purpose of the meeting is to
> consider the advisability of selling the property or of giv-
> ing it to the denomination.

And three days after the meeting, the *Journal* recorded the
outcome:

The meeting at the Baptist church Monday resulted in the church property being turned over to the state board, and from reports received, it is the intention to send a minister here and start the church again soon.[1]

While the Baptist Convention leaders were searching for a minister, three elderly ladies from the congregation were praying for one. That is when Howard's request arrived at the convention office.

THE PASTOR OF PERRY

After classes concluded in May of 1930, the Sugdens traveled back to Michigan with an invitation to preach in Perry. On Sunday, June 21, Howard took a screwdriver and pried open the front door of the church building. He entered the musty foyer and rang the bell to alert the community that the church was open for worship. And they came, a total of seven people, consisting of the three praying ladies, Howard and Lucile, and two trustees. Lucile played the piano for the service, the Sugdens sang a duet, and Howard preached. For one Sunday at least, the church was officially opened.

The *Perry Journal* tells us that "following this service a meeting of the board of trustees was held and it was unanimous to have Rev. Sugden for the regular pastor."[2] The Sugdens accepted the hasty call and by the end of the week had moved into the white clapboard parsonage next to the church. The *Journal* explained that the parsonage had just "been painted and many alterations made including a complete three-piece bathroom."[3]

On the first official Sunday, July 6, 1930, morning worship

was scheduled for 10:30, with Sunday School at 11:30, and the evening service at 8:00. For his opening message, Howard preached from Matthew 13. His sermon was entitled, "The Parable of the Hearer."[4]

"Now what are we going to do?" Lucile questioned Howard after that first Sunday. They were in charge of a congregation of seven, with little resources. The prospects were disheartening. "We are going to work. We are going to call on every house in the neighborhood. Then we are going to call on every house in town. Then we are going to call on every house on every farm. We are going to work!"[5] And that is exactly what he did!

One of the most notable characteristics of Howard's entire ministry was his belief in and his insatiable desire for work. He modeled his ministry after one of his spiritual heroes, G. Campbell Morgan. "When asked the secret of his (Morgan's) success as an interpreter of the Word, he would say, 'Work—hard work—and again, work!' He himself was in his study at 6 a.m., and he never permitted anyone to interrupt him before lunch."[6]

Howard was filled with the freshness and enthusiasm of youth. The Sugdens had little by way of human resources, but they had faith in a great God and believed that He would supply their needs through prayer. A quotation from the pen of the prolific John Newton, a favorite of Howard's, was appropriate for the situation:

> *Thou art coming to a King*
> *Large petitions with thee bring*
> *For His grace and power are such,*
> *None can ever ask too much.*[7]

EARLY PREACHING

The young pastor had his first charge and he was thrilled. From the very beginning of his ministry, Howard was a commanding presence in the pulpit. He appeared confident and spoke with authority. His preaching was dramatic, in the style of the early twentieth-century orators, and his messages were filled with imagination, grounded in simple Bible stories.

But although he appeared outwardly confident, inwardly he was insecure. His sermons lacked theological depth, and he knew it. His grammar still was unacceptable. "His sermons were better than nothing", Lucile later admitted, "and while the parents were helped, the children seemed to love it."[8] But Howard was not satisfied.

Due to his feeling of inadequacy, he asked his wife to critique his Sunday sermons. Lucile, willing to help out wherever she could, would sit in the front row every week and record anything she deemed improper from the morning message, grammatical or otherwise. After the service, she would share these observations with Howard, but only after she gave him a good Sunday dinner.[9]

It is interesting to note that Lucile continued this practice of correcting her husband throughout his ministry. The corrections became more theological over time. This exercise, however, was never carried out in a demeaning manner. In later years, to the amusement of many, the corrections would come even while Howard was speaking![10] Needless to say, this behavior was shocking to the uninitiated.

ORDINATION

After four months of ministry in Perry, Howard traveled

back to his home church to be ordained for the gospel ministry. On November 7, 1930, the small church of Mills Memorial in Mayville was filled with friends and family. Some thirty-seven delegates from surrounding churches participated in the Council. He ably defended his doctrinal beliefs and his call to the ministry before the Council. The vote to confirm Howard was unanimous. He was now an ordained minister. The ordination sermon "Preach the Word," was delivered by the pastor of the Mayville church, Rev. Henry A. Buell.[11] Howard took this stirring challenge to heart and faithfully followed it for over sixty years!

DEPRESSION DAYS

The State Convention sent the Sugdens to Perry as home missionaries with a promise of twenty-five dollars a week support. However, the promised support was not forthcoming due to the great depression that was ravaging the entire nation. The Sugdens ended up living on seven dollars and fifty cents per week, out of which they placed seventy-five cents in the offering and trusted God to supply their needs. They were driven to their knees, for they had nowhere else to turn for help. As always, God was faithful.

One time when there was no money to purchase wood for heating the stove, the Sugdens cast themselves upon the goodness of God. After committing the matter to the Lord in prayer, they heard a knock at the door. "I was passing through the area and just thought that maybe you could use some wood," said the man standing at the door. Howard replied, "Could we ever! I'll help you unload!" After the wood was neatly stacked and proper thanks had been given to the generous man, Howard and Lucile wept with joy over God's immediate provision for their need.[12]

God met their financial needs in various ways. The Walter Darling family lived next door. They were leaders in the community, owning several of the stores in town. Walter's young son, Don, struggled with reading and was doing poorly in school because of this deficiency. Lucile, without any thought of compensation, gave of her time to tutor the young boy. His progress was amazing. To express their appreciation, the Darlings gave meat and pies to the Sugdens. Howard and Lucile recognized this as a sign of God's great love for them and his promise "to supply their every need" (Philippians 4:19). Walter Darling was eventually led to Christ by Howard.

In later years Don Darling became a builder and worked with the Sudan Interior Mission, helping missionaries build homes in Africa. Sixty years later he stopped in Lansing unexpectedly to see Mrs. Sugden and thank her once again for helping a young boy learn how to read![13]

Howard instituted a Question and Answer time as a regular feature in the church life at Perry. He placed a question box near the back of the sanctuary where anyone could submit a question regarding the Bible. He would then answer these questions during an evening service.[14] This format was used with much success throughout his ministry. Rarely did he teach a Sunday School class without leaving time for Q & A. It was not surprising then, when in 1987, Howard and Lucile co-authored a book in a Question and Answer format.[15]

MINISTRY IMPACT

In spite of his inexperience and obvious educational deficiencies, Howard enjoyed the blessing of God on his ministry. Much of his success, from a human standpoint, can be attributed to the fact that he loved people. Some people in the ministry might have great relational skills but their homiletic skills are lacking. For others it is the reverse. Howard was blessed with both. He adored people and was an able expositor of the Word. When asked, "What is the secret to pastoral effectiveness?" an aged minister replied, "Simply love the people and preach the Word." Howard wholeheartedly embraced that well-proven philosophy.

Pastor Sugden was invited frequently to speak for chapel at the local high school. During his five-year ministry in Perry, he spoke at five baccalaureate services. On June 8, 1933 the *Perry Journal* observed:

> The Methodist Church was filled to capacity Sunday evening for the Perry High School Baccalaureate exercises. The Rev. Howard Sugden of the Perry Baptist Church gave one of the most masterful Baccalaureate addresses we have ever heard in Perry. It was interesting, educational, inspirational, and a very impressive and thoughtful talk, and we are sure the class of 1933 and the entire congregation could not help but receive some benefit from the many good thoughts he expressed.

A brief summary of this sermon, THE FOUR SECRETS OF JOAB'S SUCCESS, was printed in the local paper. The following transcript is the oldest record of a Sugden sermon. Howard was twenty-six years old:

There is a portion of scripture in 2 Samuel 5:8 that I

would call your attention to tonight. "Whosoever getteth up the waterspout and smiteth the Jebusites, and the lame and the blind, that are hated of David's soul, he shall be chief and captain." When David found himself king of Israel, his first desire was to have for a capital a city of importance. Jerusalem was chosen but it was occupied by the Jebusites and so well fortified that it seemed impregnable. So certain were the Jebusites of the safety of their city that they had placed the lame and the blind on the walls to guard it. David offered to the man who was able to get up the waterspout into the city the place of captain of the army of Israel. Archaeologists tell us that this waterspout was the means of Jerusalem's water supply. Joab, one of the young men of the army, was first to accept, and after what must have been a very difficult time he gained the city.

What was the secret of success? I shall refer you to four things upon which his success depended.

1. Determination—It has been said, "Put an idea on two feet and bid it travel across the continent and it will revolutionize it." Determination knows no obstacles, it discovered America, it laid the Atlantic cable after it had broken six times, and it has given to us practically every worthwhile invention. Well did the Son of God say, "No man having put his hand to the plow and looking back is fit for the kingdom of God."

2. Courage—It took courage for Joab to make the climb into the city, but if we are to take the strongholds, an equal amount of courage will be demanded of us. Joseph, one of the outstanding characters of the Old

Testament, became one of the leading figures in the land of Egypt because of his courage to stand for the things that were right. The success of Gladstone, the grand old man, has been attributed to his remarkable courage.

3. Sacrifice—The true measure of man is his willingness to sacrifice. The great apostle Paul is an outstanding example of this. He was trained in all the wisdom of his day and was able to command the attention of all, yet he was willing to sacrifice all that he might gain Christ.

4. Faith—

Were I so tall to reach the pole
And grasp the ocean in my span.
I must be measured by my soul
For 'tis the faith that makes the man.

First of all, one must have faith in himself. It was Archimedes who said, "Give me a place to stand and I'll move the world." The apostle Paul said, "I can do all things through Christ which strengtheneth me."

Then I would caution you lest you gain the stronghold and lose your own soul, because without faith in God this is the result. I would urge you tonight to place your faith in God in whom we live, move, and have our being and then we have this assurance, regardless of what life's vicissitudes may be, we can face them calmly because our life is hid in the Christ of God.

Let us remember to never give up this task of taking the strongholds; but remember the words of the poet:

Heights by great men reached and kept
Were not attained by sudden flight,
But they while their companions slept
Were toiling upward in the night.[16]

SPECIAL MEETINGS

Throughout the years, Howard brought to the Perry pulpit some excellent preachers. The man who had led him to Christ six years before, P. H. Kadey, held evangelistic meetings. Later, the Scottish team of William Mackie and Robert Irvine conducted a series of profitable services.

The largest crowds, however, gathered to hear H. H. Savage. The man who had such a powerful impact on Howard during the days immediately following his conversion now came as a mentor and co-laborer in the gospel. He spoke at least three times in Perry. On a Thursday night in September of 1933, his third visit to the church, the sanctuary was packed to capacity. The noted radio preacher spoke on "The Need for Personal Righteousness in America." His text was Proverbs 14:14, and the service was memorable.[17]

Other ministry opportunities kept Howard busy. The Annual Michigan Baptist Sunday School Convention was held at Perry in 1933. Not only did Howard host the event, he led the singing and sang two duets with Lucile. During this time, he also served as the vice-president of the Shiawassee County Sunday School Council.[18]

In July of 1932, Howard began a radio ministry over WMBC in Lapeer, Michigan. Although the program was short-lived, he loved the experience. In all of his later pastorates, this medium would play a vital role in his strategy of spreading the gospel of Christ.

BACK TO SCHOOL

Having spent only one year in Knoxville, Howard and Lucile returned to Johnson Bible College for part of the 1932–33 academic year. The Convention provided a temporary replacement for Howard in Perry while he was away. Immediately upon returning, he not only resumed his duties at the church, he began serving a second church, the Corunna Baptist Church, some twenty miles away. For over a year, he preached in both congregations every Sunday morning, while the Perry congregation remained his primary ministry.

In 1931 Howard enrolled in a summer seminary program at the Winona Lake School of Theology (the forerunner of Grace Theological Seminary in Indiana). This program was under the direction of Dr. William Pettingill: an editorial staff member of the original Scofield Reference Bible, pastor of twenty-five years in Wilmington, Delaware, author of numerous books and articles, and Dean of the Philadelphia School of the Bible. The Sugdens traveled to Winona Lake for six weeks every summer. They would take two weeks of their vacation and stay in Indiana. During the other four weeks they would drive back and forth to Perry—a 300-mile round trip—to lead the Sunday and Wednesday services.

At first Lucile was only auditing the classes because they did not have sufficient funds to pay for her tuition. She quickly came to the conclusion that this was not right! She was doing as much work as anyone else in the class but was receiving no credit for it. So she took in two boarders, who stayed in an extra bedroom in the parsonage. She would cook and do the laundry for her tenants, receiving five dollars each week for her services. With this money, she was able to pay for her tuition and become a fully accredited student at the seminary.

Ministry in Perry had gone very well. Now the Sugdens were sensing that they had accomplished all they could in the small village. When they came to Perry, the doors were bolted and the church was empty. When they left five years later, the church was full. Regular attendance Sunday morning had reached 150 people. They began praying for God's direction, and that is when the call came from Jackson, a larger city in Michigan with more opportunities for ministry.

On June 16, 1935, the Sugdens said a tearful good-bye to their first congregation.

END NOTES

1. *Perry Journal.* Perry, Michigan; February 6, 1930.

2. *Perry Journal.* Perry, Michigan; July 3, 1930.

3. Ibid.

4. Ibid.

5. Personal interview with Lucile Sugden, June 2001.

6. Jill Morgan. *A Man of the Word.* Grand Rapids: Baker; reprinted 1972, p. 325.

7. John Newton. *Trinity Hymnal.* Philadelphia: Great Commission; 1961, hymn number 531.

8. Personal interview with Lucile Sugden, October 2002.

9. Personal interview with Lucile Sugden, June 2001.

10. This usually did not happen in a normal church service, but was a frequent occurrence at Bible conferences. The regular attendees delighted in this loving banter between husband and wife.

11. *These Forty Years of Ministry*. Published by South Baptist Church, Lansing, Michigan; 1970.

12. Personal interview with Lucile Sugden, June 2001.

13. Ibid.

14. *Perry Journal*. Perry, Michigan; June 6, 1932.

15. Howard and Lucile Sugden. *What Does the Bible Say About . . . ?* Grand Rapids: Kregel; 1987.

16. *Perry Journal*. Perry, Michigan; June 8, 1933.

17. *Perry Journal*. Perry, Michigan; September 7, 1933.

18. *Perry Journal*. Perry, Michigan; October 12, 1933.

CHAPTER 4

GROWTH AT GANSON

God holds the key of all unknown, and I am glad;
If other hands should hold the key,
Or if he trusted it to me,
I might be sad.
—J. Parker

MEMBERSHIP at the Ganson Street Church was hovering around 100 people when the Sugdens arrived in the summer of 1935. Actually, they moved from a slightly larger congregation in Perry to a smaller one in Jackson. But the opportunities of a larger city, with greater potential to spread the gospel, made the invitation desirable. And besides, they would receive a salary increase of thirty-three percent! Instead of fifteen dollars a week they now would receive twenty dollars! The Sugdens felt greatly blessed indeed.

HARD AT WORK

Hard work was one of the major keys to success in the Perry ministry, and Howard had every intention of working just as hard in Jackson. When asked how he would begin his ministry at Ganson Street, he confidently replied, "We will call on as many people as we possibly can." One lady was a bit hesitant to give her support to such an aggressive proposal. She was the

56

treasurer of the church and, in one sense, ran most everything. When Howard announced that he expected a large turnout to go calling the following Saturday, the treasurer responded rather tersely, "This church has been here for fifty years and people know where it is, if they want to come, they will find us! You don't need to go after them." Howard's determination quickly overcame her reluctance. "We are going to call on as many people as we possibly can!" And the church followed his bold leadership.[1]

Having been nurtured and encouraged by the radio ministry of Henry Savage in the late 1920s, Howard had a growing desire to use this means of communication as well. Being unable to sustain a radio ministry in Perry only made the possibility of having one in Jackson a more inviting prospect. His passion for radio could now be matched with the resources of Jackson to make this "hi-tech" ministry a reality. After a few months of getting acquainted with the congregation, Howard initiated a radio broadcast of the Sunday morning services. Shortly thereafter, he began an additional weekly broadcast called "Songs In the Night." This early broadcast bore immediate fruit. Lucile remembers:

We had a man telephone us. He said, "I heard the message (on the radio) and it is something I need." My husband got his name and we went to his house. He was a doctor who was battling with alcohol. "I need what you have," he said to Howard. I remember, I went with him and we prayed with this doctor and he accepted the Lord. He had been living with a woman and they were not married. She came to the Lord. After that, they got married! He never drank again. He became one of our best men![2]

Since the church was small and the Sugdens were the only paid staff, they became heavily involved in most every facet of church life, including the youth group. Lucile would teach the young people in their weekly Bible class. Both the Sugdens would play the role of youth sponsors on weekend retreats and trips to Christian camps. In their spare time, they directed the annual Summer Bible School. This outreach ministry was the highlight of the year, with attendance eventually reaching almost 800 children. Every moment of every day was jam-packed with ministry. Howard could not have been more pleased. His constant philosophy was, "The busier the better!"

The picture of Howard Sugden that develops during the Jackson years is that of a young minister who could not say "No." Since the Sugdens had no children of their own to care for, they cared for the children of the church. Because the church lacked adequate workers, they filled many different roles. In addition, this was an era when the paid staff was expected to do most of the work. So the Sugdens did the work of the ministry—all of it! Howard did not want to disappoint his new congregation, nor did he want to disappoint his Heavenly Father! As the son of a farmer, hard work was all he knew. As a man who was well acquainted with the persistent pangs of insecurity, he labored to compensate for those feelings. He worked relentlessly to achieve and succeed in the ministry, and he did.

With his wife ministering by his side, the thirty-year-old preacher labored seven days a week without a break, week in and week out. His daily schedule would begin at 7 a.m., with a pause just before suppertime. After a brief break for supper, he would spend his evenings either ministering outside the home or studying theological literature. Even on his vacations he worked, spending much of the time speaking at Bible conferences. If "burnout" had been invented back then, Howard would have been a prime candidate for it.

Workaholism, born out of the strength of his devotion to God and his love for his congregation, apparently was a weakness he either did not recognize or one he chose to ignore. Constant work was viewed as a virtue, not a vice, in 1940. Howard always would counsel other pastors to take a day off and spend it with their families, but Lucile would later admit, "It was something he never did himself."[3] Someone has said, "Even the best of men are men at best" and we cannot expect our heroes to be without their flaws.

PREACHING

Howard's ability to proclaim God's Word was increasing. The local Jackson paper, the *Citizen Patriot*, carried this short excerpt from a Sugden sermon on Galatians 4:4:

"When the fullness of time was come, God sent forth His Son. . . ." The cross was not an afterthought in the mind of God. Before the mountains were brought forth, or even the stars shone in their splendor, in the heart of God, the cross was foreordained and Christ stood as a Lamb slain. Frequent glimpses of this truth are found in the inspired record of the Old Testament. Isaac saw the cross in the lamb, which took his place. The children of Israel saw the cross in the lamb that wrought deliverance from the bondage of Pharaoh. Isaiah saw the cross as he stood in the temple, and thus he could write, "The Lord hath laid on him the iniquity of us all." John the Baptist saw Christ and cried, "Behold the lamb of God which taketh away the sin of the world." On Calvary's cross, the Lord Jesus became the fulfillment of Old Testament prophecies and types. It was on that cross that "He who knew no sin was made sin for us, that we might be made the righteousness of God in Him." Well did the hymn writer say:

> In the cross of Christ I'll glory, towering o'er the wrecks of time,
> All the light of sacred story gathers 'round His head sublime.[4]

Howard, who never suffered from lack of imagery in preaching, began to add the solid doctrine of the Scriptures to his vivid messages. His sermons were often focused on the greatness of God or, as in the illustration above, the glorious theme of the cross. Rarely would he preach without using a quotation from a well-known hymn or some appropriate poem. An orator of no small skill had clearly emerged.

FAITHFUL HELPER

During 1940, a fruitful partnership began that lasted for over fifty years. Doris Seger, one of the young ladies from the youth group at Ganson Street, went away to college, but soon returned home with some major physical challenges. While she was recuperating, Howard asked Doris if she might help out in the office performing various secretarial tasks. She began to assist in a part-time capacity, but her value became immediately apparent. Soon she found herself in the full-time employment of the church as the pastor's personal secretary. A close bond developed between the Sugdens and Doris; she was accepted as part of the family, like the child they never had. Doris quickly learned Howard's strengths and areas of weakness and devoted herself to making her pastor even more effective. They shared a mutual love of books and often would discuss various authors and writings that had nourished their faith. Doris also learned the art of working not only with the pastor but with Lucile as well. Simply being successful in the former did not necessarily guarantee success in the latter. Together they formed a three-fold cord that would not be easily broken.

Doris became such a valuable asset to Howard's ministry that when the Sugdens left Jackson to move to Canada in 1951 she moved with them and continued to be Howard's secretary. Three years later, when the Sugden family made their final ministry move, this time to Lansing, Michigan, Howard's acceptance was contingent on the employment of Doris as well. Faithful people are difficult to find (Proverbs 2:6), and when Howard found Doris, he would not let her go!

THEOLOGICAL TRAINING CONTINUES

While in Jackson, the Sugdens continued their trips to Winona Lake for theological study each summer. It took them eleven summers—sixty-six weeks of work—until they graduated in May of 1941. Through perseverance, Howard and Lucile earned their Bachelor of Religious Education degrees. The man who had fooled his way through high school had now graduated from a theological institution. Howard had developed into a conscientious student. Some began to call him a self-made scholar.

BLESSINGS AND BATTLES

The ministry at Ganson Street was expanding. Three building programs were launched, including the construction of a larger auditorium. Some estimated that the growth of the church was almost ten-fold, with attendance reaching 1,000 people.[5]

The Lord was using Howard and Lucile to win many to Christ. Years later, while preaching on the Philippian jailer, Howard remembers one such conversion:

> When Mrs. Sugden and I went to Jackson for the first time, a lovely, gracious lady came to me that first morning. Quietly, she laid her tender hands on my shoulders and said to me, "Could I ask you to do something for me? My husband is the deputy warden of the Jackson Prison. He never comes to church. He doesn't have any time for God. He runs the prison with an iron hand. If somebody does something wrong, he'll grab them by the neck and spit in their face." Deputy McCoy was a feared man. She said, "Would you go and see him?" I went to see him. When he was at home I would go out and see him, [and] give him a hug. You know what happened? One day he got saved! That caused a revolution in Jackson Prison more than anything. He went back to the prison, went to the men whose faces he had spit upon, and asked for their forgiveness. Just like the Philippian jailer.[6]

Some growing pains, however, could not be avoided. A conflict surfaced with the Michigan Baptist Convention. The denomination had a strong ecclesiastical hold over the Jackson congregation. Before the church could proceed with any remodeling or building addition, they had to receive authorization from the convention and give the deed of the property to the denomination. Feeling that such control was too high-handed, Howard took the issue to the church. Emotional ties to the convention were strong and disagreements ensued. But in the end, the church voted to withdraw from the convention, and become independent. Howard maintained a positive relationship with many different organizations, but he remained denominationally unconnected for the rest of his ministry. He valued his ecclesiastical freedom. He was convinced that the danger of denominational abuse far outweighed the benefits derived from membership.[7]

A FAMILY

By the end of 1949, the Sugdens had been married twenty-one years, but they had no children. Although they craved a family, they were resigned to the fact that the Lord must have other plans for them. It was, of course, most difficult for Lucile. She bravely continued giving herself to two ministries, teaching the Bible and caring for Howard. Yet such resignation did not eliminate the strong desire to raise children.

In 1950, the Sugdens heard about the hardship a young family was experiencing in their city. An alcoholic and abusive husband had abandoned his family and left his wife to care for their three children. A loving grandmother, who attended Howard's church, stepped in to do what she could for this fatherless brood, but her resources were small.

When Howard heard the story his heart was deeply touched. He asked the mother if she would allow him to adopt the children. Lucile's sister, who lived nearby, was childless as well and wondered if she might be able to adopt one or two of the children. After a terrible struggle, the mother concluded that her children would be better off with the Sugdens. So Lucile's sister adopted Judy and David. Howard and Lucile lovingly adopted Sylvia. At ten years of age, Sylvia was the oldest of the three children.

What an immediate change it was for all parties. Everything was different for Sylvia. She had never lived in a Christian family, and now she was living in a pastor's home! She became a "P. K." overnight and wasn't sure she liked it. Her frustration was mounting. "It seems like all we do is go to church . . . it's not easy being a preacher's kid! Everyone expects you to be perfect!"[8] Acting like a Christian was hard, being perfect—that was out of the question!

The change in the Sugden's life was a challenge as well. Most every day Howard would rearrange his schedule to drive Sylvia to school. As she would get out of the car, Howard would say, "You know I love you!" Every night he would tenderly tuck his new daughter into bed. With hearts full of loving compassion, Howard and Lucile tried to reach out to Sylvia, but they could see that she was hurting. The road of adjustment would be long.

MINISTRY INFLUENCE

Howard's ministry began to expand far beyond the city limits of Jackson and the walls of the Ganson Street Church. If his ministry in Perry was where he got his theological feet wet, in Jackson he began to swim quite a distance from shore. Lucile used to say, "He developed as a preacher in Jackson, but he didn't get real good until he went to Canada!"[9] The crowds that gathered each Sunday to hear his unique preaching thought he was pretty good right then!

With his commitment to hard work in the study, his dramatic oratorical style in the pulpit, and his own church averaging about 1,000 every Sunday, Howard Sugden was making a name for himself. To be sure, this was not his intention, but it was a reality. Howard was in demand! Bible conferences and pastors' fellowships were asking him to speak at their conventions. Throughout the week, Howard would often travel from Jackson to small congregations in Ohio, Michigan, and Indiana to hold gospel services. Further trips took him to Canada, New England, and the West Coast. The Executive Secretary of a New England Fellowship said, "The pastors of New England, I believe, would give testimony with me that one of the greatest contributions to their spiritual lives has been through the ministry of Howard Sugden."[10]

The Ganson ministry became an ever-widening influence for Howard Sugden. He had been in Jackson for sixteen years, through the difficult war years, and the congregation was healthy and happy. The church was doing well and attracting attention. Human measurements of success were everywhere to be found. And that is why a church came calling from London, Ontario, Canada.

END NOTES

1. Personal interview with Lucile Sugden, June 2001.

2. Personal interview with Lucile Sugden, November 2001.

3. Personal interview with Lucile Sugden, June 2001.

4. The *Citizen Patriot*. Jackson, Michigan; April 1938.

5. *These Forty Years of Ministry*. Published by South Baptist Church, Lansing, Michigan; 1970.

6. Howard Sugden. *A Call to Advance*. A sermon delivered at South Baptist Church, Lansing, Michigan; January 24, 1988.

7. Personal interview with Lucile Sugden, November 2001.

8. Ibid.

9. Personal interview with Lucile Sugden, June 2001.

10. *These Forty Years of Ministry*. Published by South Baptist Church, Lansing, Michigan; 1970.

CHAPTER 5

FOREIGN EXCHANGE

What on earth have we gotten ourselves into?
—*Howard F. Sugden*

IN April of 1951, the Sugdens exchanged sixteen years of fruitful ministry in Jackson for an unknown future in a foreign land. Howard had just turned forty-four years old when he moved his family to Canada. By this time he had become a well-known pastor and leader in fundamental-evangelical circles throughout North America. Several different churches were clamoring for his services. After much prayer, he and Lucile made the difficult decision to accept the call from Central Baptist Church of London, Ontario.

This was a major move. Special permission had to be secured from governmental agencies regarding the adoption of Sylvia, which had not yet been finalized. The move would also involve transporting the growing library Howard had accumulated throughout the 1940s, now numbering several thousand volumes.

Leaving friends and family for a different country was daunting as well, even if that country was only a six-hour drive away. But convinced that God was guiding their steps, they tearfully said good-bye to Michigan and enthusiastically said hello to Canada.

CENTRAL BAPTIST CHURCH

A Scotsman by the name of James McGinlay was the first pastor of the Central Baptist Church, started in 1928. In 1929, the church rented out the Capitol Theatre for Sunday services. Realizing that the church could not continue in this situation for an extended period of time, McGinlay began looking for a more suitable location. That is when he discovered the beautiful three-story, redbrick Victorian house at 602 Queens Avenue in London.

The original owner of the mansion was Benjamin Cronyn Jr., who built the residence in 1864. Colonel E. Leonard purchased the home in 1890, leaving the estate to his widow when he passed away in 1923.[1] McGinlay noticed the letters B.C. carved on the doorframes throughout the mansion, the initials of the previous owner. He told the Leonard family that he was convinced this was the building for the church, since their name was already on the structure, the initials B.C. meaning Baptist Church.[2]

With logic like that, who could resist? She and her family sold the house to the church for $23,000. McGinlay had his church, a Lighthouse for London.

They gutted out the structure to transform it for church ministry. An auditorium was constructed in the mansion that would seat 700 people, having a balcony that wrapped around the entire sanctuary, with stairs that descended from the gallery to the central platform. An annex was added both to the east and to the north to provide sufficient Sunday school and administrative space for the growing church. The famous pastor, T. T. Shields from Jarvis Street Baptist Church, Toronto, spoke at the dedication service.

ADJUSTING TO THE CULTURE

"We thought Canada would be similar to America, but we soon found out that it was different, very English," said Lucile. "I remember the first day after we moved in. Howard was walking down the street when he met a lady and, in his friendly way, said 'Good Morning.' She turned around and tersely replied, 'Sir, we have never met!' He came home and said to me, 'What on earth have we gotten ourselves into?'"[3]

Howard's plan of ministry was the same as it had been in America, to personally call in the homes of the people throughout the community. To his surprise, he learned that unannounced visits were frowned upon in Canada. He also learned that any home visit he did make became an extended social occasion, especially when he had to stay for tea.

Lucile thoroughly enjoyed Canadian life, but Howard had a harder time.[4] His flamboyant ways and American friendliness would be often tested during his time north of the border.

LEGALISM IN LONDON

James McGinlay started the Central Church on a foundation of very strict ideas. For instance, he vowed that the church building would never have a kitchen and the worship services would never feature a choir.[5] Other personal opinions became guiding convictions for the life of the church. Subtly, a spirit of legalism began to take hold.

Dr. S. Franklin Logsdon followed McGinlay at Central. He left London to follow the well-known H. A. Ironside as pastor of the equally famous Moody Memorial Church in Chicago. Logsdon's move to Chicago proved to be misguided—he lasted only eighteen months. Dr. Logsdon had a good ministry in

London for nine years, but he was a very staid and dignified man who did little to change the legalistic tendencies of the church. Lucile recalls a godly woman who had a tremendous testimony in the community, but was looked upon with suspicion within the church due to a divorce she experienced prior to her conversion. The deacons would not allow her to participate in any ministry. Harsh policies, built on distorted views of separation from sin can restrict freedom of ministry in the body of Christ and negatively affect any outreach to those who are without Christ. Lucile comments:

> We believed in separation *from* the world, but we also believed it comes from being separated to Christ. If you are separated to Christ, your mind and your heart will be filled with the Spirit and your attitude toward the world will take care of itself. We are responsible for our own spiritual lives; we are not responsible to judge others. More churches have been split by legalism than anything else. My husband expounded the Word of God. He felt he had no business telling people what to do. He was responsible to get the Word of God to them, but they had to follow it. The Word of God is very plain about salvation and the Christian life. People must read the Word of God and do it, not because they are told to by an outside force, not because of duty, but because of their relationship to Jesus Christ and their love for Him.[6]

A PREACHER WITH POWER

When the Sugdens arrived in 1951, the church was averaging around 800 people on a Sunday. However, the ministry at Central was in need of much encouragement and leadership. When the Sugdens left the church three years later, attendance was approaching 1100 and the Sunday school had registered a high of 1300. Even more importantly, the congregation was unified and enthusiastic about its ministry for God.[7]

Lucile believed that Howard's preaching grew dramatically while in London. The reason for this, in her estimation, was the close proximity of the London Bible Institute to their church.[8] With the Institute only a block away, many of the students made Central their church home. The presence of these serious Bible students challenged Howard to go deeper into the Scriptures than he had ever gone before.

The Sugdens enjoyed a wonderful relationship with the Institute. Not only did the students attend their church, Howard and Lucile both regularly taught in the school. Howard lectured on Pastoral Theology and Homiletics, and Lucile was an instructor in Christian Education for Women and Youth. Howard also served briefly as a member of the Board of Directors.[9]

Howard's preaching ministry in Canada was warmly received. However, it was not without its challenges. One challenge was cultural. In a sermon on Sunday morning, Howard referred to a small child as a "cute little bugger." To his chagrin he was made aware of the fact the word *bugger* was highly offensive to Canadian ears. He was kindly warned to be more careful about his word choice in the future.[10]

Another challenge came in the form of a wealthy businessman in the church. Although this individual held no official position, he did wield a lot of influence among the congregants.

He was quite gifted in causing considerable dissension among the people of God. Feeling duty bound to exercise his significant gift on his pastor, he frequently opposed Howard. Howard could not appease this critic and the verbal wounds he received were felt deeply.[11] We don't know if Paul's thorn in the flesh was a physical problem or a relational difficulty (2 Corinthians 12:7). Howard's thorn was very much in the flesh!

Pastor Sugden's preaching, which was already powerful, took on a new dimension. His personal study time in the Word intensified. The content of his preaching became more doctrinally based, permeated with the meat of the Word. Before he went to London, his sermons were twenty to twenty-five minutes in length. As they became deeper in content, they lengthened in time. In London his average sermon was thirty-five to forty minutes long. His style, however, remained overtly dramatic! He knew how to work an audience with his voice, keeping it very low and sustained, and then raising the pitch and volume to grab the attention of his audience. This was confirmed one day when, at the corner store, a little boy who attended Central Baptist came up to Howard and said, "I know you! You're the man who hollers in church!"[12]

Howard's dramatic style sometimes had a very magnetic effect on his congregation. While preaching on David and Goliath, Howard told the ancient story with such vivid imagery that the people actually felt they were in the valley of Elah. The west balcony, according to Howard, was the camp of Israel. The east balcony was the camp of the Philistines. The main floor was the valley where David confronted Goliath. As Howard would describe the camp of the Israelites, he would motion with his hand to the balcony on the west, and all heads in the auditorium would turn to the west, as though by looking they could see the tents. As he talked about the camp of the Philistines, he would point to the east balcony, and all heads would turn to the east. One has to wonder if Howard saw the difficult business-man sitting among the Philistines! When he referred to the actual battle between David and Goliath in the valley of Elah, it was said that some of the people in the galleries got out of their seats to peer over the rails and watch the fight unfold! The impact of that familiar story told in a fresh and living manner is still remembered fifty years later![13]

Dr. Ed Matthews, a chief administrator in the public schools of London, who also served as Sunday School Superintendent and deacon in the church, observed:

> One cannot overlook the exceptional characteristics of Pastor Sugden's pulpit ministry. Always his messages centered on God's blessed Word, giving evidence of hours of prayerful, searching study which enables him to translate the spiritual truths of the Word into day-by-day Christian living in a most unusual manner. Enriched by the liberal use of apt illustrations and picturesque language, his presentation of the Word is forceful and dynamic.[14]

One of the great blessings of the ministry at Central was the emergence and growth of a Sunday night service, due in no small part to Howard's preaching. Many churches in the sur-rounding area did not have a Sunday night service, and those that did often struggled to find an audience. Howard focused on evangelism, advertised heavily, and encouraged his people to bring others with them each Sunday night. Consequently, the church was filled with many individuals who were not regular Sunday morning attendees.

Howard's outside speaking ministry continued to expand while in Canada. He spoke at the New Brunswick Bible Institute and often was a featured speaker at the regular meetings of the Fellowship Baptists of Canada. His relationship with Canadian Keswick grew stronger. Howard normally spent two weeks in ministry every summer at Keswick, now he was spending four. In February of 1954, he was one of the keynote speakers at Moody Founders Week, delivering a series of messages on five Old Testament characters.[15]

A PREACHER WITH HEART

If it was Howard's gift of preaching that created the crowds, it was his love that kept them coming back. A visitor, who looked a little out of place, began attending every Sunday night. Howard made it a point to give the man a warm embrace and say, "I'm glad you're here!" But strangely, although the man's eyes would fill with tears, he never said a word. He came Sunday after Sunday without speaking to Howard, but would always receive the same warm hug and kind words. Finally, the man stopped coming.

Six years later, when Howard was speaking during a morning session at Canadian Keswick, he looked up and saw that familiar face, the silent Sunday night visitor. Immediately after the meeting, Howard went to the back to see the gentleman and asked, "Are you the man that used to come to the Central Baptist Church in London several years ago? You came every Sunday night for many months, and then disappeared . . . are you the same man?"

"Yes, that was me!" the man acknowledged. "And did you ever wonder why I never spoke to you?"

Howard replied, "Yes, I was always curious about that."

"Well, I had just come from Denmark to Canada when I found your church and attended your evening service. I did not know one word of English, so I could not speak to you."

Puzzled, Howard asked, "But you came back every Sunday night for months. Why did you come if you could not understand the message?"

The man replied, "I came back for your hug!"

The universal language of a warm smile and a loving hug brought the man from Denmark back Sunday after Sunday. He never understood the sermons, but he never forgot the hug![16]

Howard loved to go through the auditorium prior to a service and greet people individually, especially at the evening service. This "working the crowd" was something he had perfected back in Jackson. However, this method of pastoral visitation took some adjustment for his Canadian audience. They had never seen it done before! Normally, people prepared their hearts in silence prior to the service—there was no talking or visiting. Over time, however, Howard's loving ways won their hearts. When the Lord called the Sugdens back to the United States, one individual said, "We are sure going to miss your visits on Sunday nights!"[17]

AMAZING GRACE!

One of the most exciting events that transpired during the London ministry happened in Howard's family. The schools in Canada were very different from the schools in America, far more strict and regimented. Sylvia had major adjustments to make. She was learning to live in a pastor's family, and now she had to adjust to a foreign country. Thankfully, she made good progress. She found the schools to her liking and excelled in athletics. Sylvia fit into the culture famously.

But the most exciting change took place during a service in 1953. At the conclusion of an evening evangelistic meeting, 13 year-old Sylvia came down the stairs from the balcony to the main platform to give her heart to Christ, to receive Jesus as her Savior and Lord. Sylvia was now a Christian. The love and patience the Sugdens had showered upon this young girl from the troubled family had now, by the grace of God, issued forth in the birth of a new child of God.[18]

TIME TO MOVE ON

The South Baptist Church in Lansing, Michigan, was having its struggles. They had shown interest in the young pastor from Jackson in the early 1950s, but before they could make a connection, he had been called to Canada. Nevertheless, they did not let the distance stop them. On three different occasions they asked Howard to consider coming to Lansing, and on each occasion he declined.

During the month of August 1953, while Howard was speaking at Canadian Keswick, the persistent men from South Church in Lansing again cornered him. There was something about their determination and urgent appeal that made him wonder if this might be from God! He said he would prayerfully consider their request.

As he was mulling over the Lansing offer, one of his friends, a Presbyterian pastor and leader at Keswick, stopped by for a visit. "You've come just at the right time because I'm trying to make a decision about a church in Lansing, Michigan, and I need your counsel," Howard said. "They want me to come and I've told them, 'No,' but they keep coming back! The church has had a split and things are not going well. I don't know what to do."

The wise pastor from Baltimore, said, "Do you want the will of God for your life more than anything else?" Howard replied, "Yes, I do. I really want to be in the center of God's will." "Then pray, and make your choice. God will not let you choose out of His will." That word of godly advice gave the Sugdens the peace they had been seeking. God would guide their decision through prayer.[19] And as they prayed throughout that fall, they sensed that God was leading them to Lansing.

Early in 1954, the Sugdens accepted the call to Lansing. Sylvia was devastated by the decision. She had now come to faith in Christ, and was thoroughly enjoying her friends and school situation in Canada. She did not want to return to the area where she had encountered so many difficulties as a child.

The people at Central were greatly saddened by this sudden move. The church was healthy and growing, and except for a rare businessman or two, the people loved their pastor. Besides, the Lansing situation seemed unhealthy and unattractive. South Baptist was one-fourth the size of Central Baptist, and the congregation was hurting. Why move from the happy to the hopeless?

For one thing, Howard simply felt that this was the will of God. That was his primary reason. For another, he was motivated by the choice of the best fit for future ministry. Howard retained a love affair with many things Canadian for the rest of his life. He often spoke with extreme fondness of his adopted land. But he believed that he would have a more effective ministry in the familiar climate of his homeland.

Marion Cornwall, an Assistant Primary Superintendent of the London Schools and a member of Central Baptist, spoke for the whole congregation when she remarked:

> Pastor Sugden's ministry in London was all too brief, but during his short stay he gained the respect of the community and won an honored place in the hearts of the members and adherents of Central Church. His faithful ministry of God's Word, backed by a life which "adorned the doctrine of God our Savior in all things," was an inspiration to all. A wise man once said, "Preaching is more than merely the delivery of a message, it is the outflow of a life." It is this outflow of Pastor's Sugden's life which has left a lasting imprint on the pages of Central's history. He had a keen vision for the work to be done . . . reckoning upon God to give us great victories in the unreached areas of our own lives and of our city. God did give us great victories. Pastor Sugden's Christ-centered ministry was an enriching experience for the hundreds who came to hear him week after week. As a congregation, we came to honor God's Word in a very precious way and were continually challenged with the privileges and the responsibilities of being a Christian. Yes, preaching is more than merely the delivery of a message, it is the outflow of a life. Pastor's life flowed out to others continually. He always had a sympathetic ear and an understanding heart. The work of Central Baptist Church has been enriched because God led you and your gracious

wife our way. Your ministry was characterized by sweetness, graciousness, a love, a gentleness that attracted [us] to the Lord Jesus Christ. It is only natural that our hearts were saddened as a church [when you left]. We had to bow to God's will for your life, as He led you on.[20]

A growing church in Canada, with the congregation that loved him, exchanged for a difficult situation in Lansing with a congregation that did not know him—could this move be the will of God? Yes, it was! And Howard would never move again for the rest of his life!

END NOTES

1. *A Jubilee of Blessings.* Published by Central Baptist Church, London, Ontario, for their 50th Anniversary celebration; 1978.

2. Personal interview with Lucile Sugden, November 2001.

3. Ibid.

4. Ibid.

5. Personal interview with Rev. Desmond Bell, January 2003.

6. Personal interview with Lucile Sugden, November 2001.

7. Personal interview with Rev. Desmond Bell, January 2003.

8. Personal interview with Lucile Sugden, June 2001.

9. Personal interview with Lucile Sugden, November 2001.

10. Personal interview with Rev. Desmond Bell, January 2003.

11. Ibid.

12. Marion Cornwall. *This Is Your Life.* A presentation at South Baptist Church, Lansing, Michigan; March 1958.

13. Personal interview with Rev. Desmond Bell, January 2003.

14. *These Forty Years of Ministry.* Published by South Baptist Church, Lansing, Michigan; 1970.

15. Howard spoke on the following subjects: Jacob, the Man With A Limp; Joseph, the Man In Whom the Spirit of God Is; Moses, the Man Who Saw God Face to Face; Elijah, the Man of God; and Daniel, A Man Greatly Beloved.

16. Personal interview with Lucile Sugden, November 2001.

17. Ibid.

18. Ibid.

19. Ibid.

20. Marion Cornwall. *This Is Your Life*. A presentation at South Baptist Church, Lansing, Michigan; March 1958.

CHAPTER 6

EARLY LIFE IN LANSING

Mark the man or woman who seeks and sees something good
in everybody; there goes a magnificent soul.
—Howard F. Sugden

IN 1889, the First Baptist Church of Lansing, Michigan, started a mission on the south side of the city. Lansing, the state capital, was a thriving town of 12,000 people. Gaslights illuminated the city, and only two years earlier, a man by the name of Ransom Eli Olds, a member at First Baptist, had driven a three-wheeled, steam-powered horseless carriage out of the Engine Works on River Street. Five years later he would develop the first gasoline-fired vehicle.[1] From that historic moment, Lansing would quickly emerge as one of the nation's major automobile centers.

The small mission began as a prayer meeting in May. In October, a quaint little building was constructed on South Street, and the people called the mission the South Street Chapel. Twenty years later, on February 28, 1909, the growing church moved into its beautiful new brick building just two blocks away on South Washington Avenue. The name was changed to the South Washington Avenue Baptist Church to reflect the new location. Sometime around 1912, the church became known as South Baptist, and the nickname of South Church was commonly used.

Throughout the first half of the twentieth century, and through a series of nine different pastors, the church made steady progress. However, when Pastor Malcolm Cronk resigned in 1952, the church was pastorless for two years and problems developed. The people became discouraged and restless. A sizable number of congregants broke off to form another church. Financial problems ensued and business meetings were contentious. The building was in need of repair and Sunday morning attendance dropped in half, to less than 300 people.

Although the pulpit committee from South had received three rejections from Howard previously, their persistence was finally rewarded. After much prayer, Howard told the church that he would accept the call on two conditions: one, that he would be able to bring with him his personal secretary, Doris Seger; and two, so that there would be no more fighting in the church, he asked the deacons for control of all business meetings and the authority to "call the shots." The church accepted his terms and Howard accepted their call, becoming the tenth pastor of the sixty-five-year-old congregation.[2] The *Lansing State Journal* announced:

> Rev. Howard Sugden of London, Ontario, has recently accepted a call to the pastorate of South Baptist Church and expects to begin his duties here at services April 4th, the first Sunday of the month. The new pastor is widely known throughout the United States and Canada as a Bible conference speaker and Bible teacher. His topic for his first Sunday morning service will be "Songs In the Night" and in the evening service, he will speak on "How Odd is God?"[3]

Although a blizzard greeted the Sugdens on April 4, 1954, the South congregation warmly received them. That Sunday, Howard's forty-seventh birthday, was the inauguration of an amazing ministry that would continue for over thirty-five years![4]

WORKING HARD AGAIN

The year 1954 was a busy one. Howard was still convinced that, in addition to strong biblical preaching, the best way to build a solid church was to maintain an aggressive visitation program—hard work, and more hard work. In later years, when younger pastors would ask Howard for the secret of his success, he would respond by saying, "Pray without ceasing, always count on the greatness of God, and work at least twelve hours a day."[5]

When Howard had told his dad that he wanted to be a pastor, Charles Sugden, the lifetime farmer, gave his son some wise counsel; "I have found that when the horses are working they don't kick. The same will be true of your church. Keep your people working and they won't cause trouble."[6] An intensive calling program was launched immediately and the people rallied around their new pastor.

Howard did little to moderate his workaholic ways. Since farmers were up before dawn, he felt obliged to do the same. If farmers worked seven days a week, then pastors should do no less. For a period of time, Howard even required his staff to meet on Saturday mornings![7]

The Lansing church began to explode. The Bible school reached approximately 400 that first year. An extension was quickly built onto the church for offices and classrooms. A radio broadcast began that would survive, without interruption, for thirty-five years.

In 1956, a large apartment building, two houses, and a dry cleaning plant were purchased, and then razed, to make room for a second building project—a new auditorium. The new sanctuary would seat around 900 people and was the largest religious facility in the Lansing area.[8] Some were convinced that Howard could never fill it. They would soon be proven wrong!

Dedication Sunday took place on October 28, 1956, with Howard's good friend and mentor from Pontiac, Dr. Henry H. Savage, as the guest speaker. Meetings and activities were planned from Sunday through Wednesday. Howard spoke Sunday morning on the theme "God Builds His Church." His thoughts were recorded in the Dedication Bulletin:

> It is ours today to look back over fifty years of history and to thank God for faithful men and women who labored with faithful pastors for the work of Christ in this place at the corner of South Washington and Moores River Drive. As we rejoice in the blessings of the past, our look back is a fleeting one, for we realize that as a people there rests upon us a tremendous obligation to this present generation. We believe that in the good Providence of God, He has brought us to Himself, and that it is His divine intention and purpose that we should become in this city a church known for its message and its passion—its message, the glorious Gospel of Jesus Christ, its passion, to make Him known by our lives and our personal witness. This glorious opportunity challenges us today. With our enlarged facilities we should be expecting great things from God and attempting great things for God.[9]

After preaching in Pontiac that morning, Dr. Savage arrived for the 3:00 p.m. meeting where he delivered a message entitled, "The Only True New Testament Church." That night Savage spoke again, this time on the subject, "The Future of the Church." Former staff and friends of the church joined with the members to celebrate the good things God had accomplished in their fellowship.

Five times the facility at South Baptist had to be enlarged or expanded during Howard's long ministry. Each time it was with the conviction that new goals of attendance and training should be reached. Pastor Sugden was always pressing to reach more people for Christ. "We are grateful for the devoted members and friends who make this work at South an aggressive force for the gospel in this great city."[10]

Howard's hard work was also rewarded on August 17, 1956, when he was given an honorary doctorate by Wheaton College and served as the keynote speaker during commencement. This Doctor of Divinity degree would be the first of three honorary doctorates he would receive during his lifetime. After completing his B.R.E. degree from the Winona Lake School of Theology in 1941, Howard took some classes toward a Masters degree, but never finished the program. Now Wheaton, an institution with a well-deserved reputation for academic excellence, was honoring Howard as a self-made scholar, a remarkable preacher, and an effective pastor. The farm boy from Mayville was doing all right!

LET THE LITTLE CHILDREN COME

One of the exemplary features of Howard's life and ministry was his love for children. His caring ways and kind heart were a magnet to kids of all ages. He made it a point to spend time with them. Every Sunday morning during his long ministry in Lansing, he would visit every Sunday School class, sprinting up and down the stairs of the church to reach the children before he had to teach his Sunday School class. In these brief visits he would offer kind words of greeting and encouragement. Excitedly he would say, "Good Morning!" clapping his hands together and almost bouncing with joy. "I am so glad to have you all here on this beautiful Lord's Day. Come back tonight and bring your parents!" The kids became convinced that Pastor Sugden really liked them! His enthusiasm was contagious.[11]

While in Jackson, Howard started the practice of picking up children to bring them to Sunday School. One notable little girl stands out. She came from a very poor family and lived in a deplorable house. "My house looks better from the inside looking out than it does looking in," she said. The Sugdens would transport this dear child back and forth to church each week. Many years later, while in Lansing, a young lady came up to Howard, and said, "Do you remember me? I am the little girl from Jackson that you took to church every Sunday." Howard said he did remember her and was thrilled to see her again. "I am a registered nurse now," she said, "and I just want to say 'thank you' for caring and making a difference in my life!"[12]

When Howard retired from active ministry at the age of eighty-two, a local newspaper reporter wrote: "Children hold a special place for Sugden. Many of them paid tribute to him during the retirement dinner last week. The children said, 'We love Pastor Sugden because he hugs us!' Sugden said with a smile, 'We love the children.'"[13]

Unbeknownst to many people in the Lansing church, Dr. Sugden continued his practice of picking up a carload of children to bring them to Sunday School each week. He did this without fanfare and without attention.

Driving through the city, Howard would often see a group of kids playing in a yard or walking down the street. Spontaneously he would break out in audible prayer that God would bless them and bring them to Jesus.[14]

POSITIVE CHRISTIANITY

To put it simply, Howard was positive about people! He would often say, "Mark the man or woman who seeks and sees something good in everybody; there goes a magnificent soul."[15] Doris Seger, Howard's secretary for over fifty years, said, "Pastor Sugden is really a patient and scholarly man who loves people. He always knows people are going to be better with the Lord's help. He is an optimist."[16] A long-time member recalls, "Pastor was positive, that was probably his most endearing trait. He thought so highly of us as a congregation. When he made a point of how we should act as God's people, he implied that we were already that way. Of course we knew we fell short."[17]

Howard had a wonderful way of making everyone feel like a dear friend. Even if he did not know someone, he would still converse with them in his warm way and friendly manner without any hint of unfamiliarity. As soon as the individual would leave, he would turn to Lucile and say, "Who was that?"[18]

Howard's compassion and warm personality began to pervade every facet of the Lansing ministry. Printed on the weekly bulletin was this invitation:

To all who mourn and need comfort, to all who are weary and need rest, to all who are lonely and want friendship, to all who are tired and want victory, to all who sin and need a Savior, to whosoever will, this church opens wide its doors and in the name of Jesus Christ, the Lord says, "Welcome."[19]

Howard knew that the best way to motivate people to follow the Lord was not by scolding them, but by encouraging them. While preaching at a conference in Minneapolis, Howard shared the pulpit with Dr. Alan Redpath, who had recently stepped down as Pastor of Moody Church in Chicago. Howard asked Dr. Redpath how the church was doing.

"Well, I recently sneaked in one Sunday morning and sat in the back seat. The Pastor said to congregation, 'I want to thank you dear folk for coming to the service today. You have been a blessing by being here and I want to thank you; and I want to tell you I love you.' Can you imagine that? Why, when I was at Moody Church I would end the message with either 'shape up or ship out!'"

"And what did the people do?"

"They shipped out!" Redpath said regrettably.

Howard observed, "Don't you think his way is a little better than your way?" Redpath had to agree.[20]

In March of 1958, South Baptist gave a surprise tribute to the Sugdens for their four years of service. The program followed the format of the popular 1950s television show, "This Is Your Life." A series of friends and family were paraded across the stage during the service to acknowledge the impact that Howard and Lucile had on their lives. The evening ended with the heartfelt prayer that "the Lord will give us many fruitful years together here at South. We love you and want you to know we are back of you!"[21]

A MAN IN DEMAND

Churches were constantly begging Dr. Sugden to leave Lansing and become their pastor. When he would be invited to speak, he had a hard time saying, "No." These churches were very serious about courting him, but he was not as serious about joining them. He simply enjoyed preaching the Word of God wherever or whenever the opportunity would arise. This often led to an awkward situation.

There was at least one invitation that Howard seriously considered; it came from the First Baptist Church of Pontiac. It was the late fall of 1961 when Dr. Henry Savage, Howard's dear friend and mentor, retired from thirty-eight years of fruitful ministry in Pontiac. His farewell message was planned for December 17. Dr. Savage's first choice for his replacement was Howard Sugden.

A young missionary who grew up at First Baptist Church, Bob Shelton, was filling the pulpit until a full-time pastor could be found. Bob and his family had just returned from ministry in Vietnam and were unable to go back due to the outbreak of war. Bob was on the list of candidates, well behind Howard.

Howard agreed to preach at First Baptist and meet with the board to discuss his interest in and compatibility with the Pontiac church. The first meeting went well. Several others followed, with each one eliciting greater progress toward Howard's acceptance of the church's offer. Finally, a financial package was agreed upon. The Sugdens went house hunting in the area. In the minds of the First Baptist leadership, it was a done deal! They desperately wanted Howard as their senior pastor and he was inclined to accept the call.

He left the final meeting with the trustees, promising that he would call the following week with his final decision. Howard struggled in prayer over this opportunity. He had a desire, on the one hand, to follow his friend, H. H. Savage. But what about the Lansing congregation . . . was it time to leave them after seven years of effective ministry? In the end, the Lord would not let Howard go.

Howard first called Bob Shelton and said, "Bob, the Lord told me that you should take the pastorate at First Baptist." He then called the trustees and informed them that he must decline their offer. Howard had spoken like a prophet. The leadership of First Baptist did choose Bob Shelton to be their pastor and he served the church for over twelve years.[22]

When Howard began his ministry in Lansing, he started to record the names of the people he led to Christ or helped in some specific way. At the end of thirty-five years of ministry, the book contained over 900 names. With tears in his eyes he confessed, "All the glory must go to God."[23]

Howard's source of strength for ministry can clearly be attributed to the power and blessing of God. He loved to quote Isaiah 40:31:

But those who wait on the Lord shall renew their
strength;
They shall mount up with wings like eagles,
They shall run and not be weary,
They shall walk and not faint.

But there was another source of strength, divinely given, that mightily helped him along the way.

END NOTES

1. George S. May. *R. E. Olds: Auto Industry Pioneer.* Grand Rapids: Eerdmans Publisher, 1977, p. 44–52.

2. Personal letter from Rev. Desmond Bell, February 2002.

3. *Lansing State Journal.* Lansing, Michigan; April 1, 1954. This particular sermon, How Odd is God, was a favorite of Dr. Sugden's, as he repeated it several times throughout his Lansing ministry.

4. *A Centennial Celebration.* Published by South Baptist Church, Lansing, Michigan; 1989.

5. *These Forty Years of Ministry.* Published by South Baptist Church, Lansing, Michigan; 1970.

6. Personal interview with Lucile Sugden, November 2001.

7. Personal interview with Dr. Sam Hoyt, January 2003.

8. The *Centennial Celebration* publication of 1989 states that the auditorium capacity was 1100. The Dedication Booklet for the new auditorium (1956) claims room for 1200 and a choir capacity of 70. It would have been extremely difficult to achieve these goals without very skinny people. A more realistic estimate brings the seating capacity to fewer than 900.

9. *Dedication Bulletin for the New Auditorium.* Published by South Baptist, Lansing, Michigan; October 28, 1956.

10. Ibid.

11. Personal letters from Susan Philip (March 2002) and Melissa VanCleve, (February 2002).

12. Personal interview with Lucile Sugden, June 2001.

13. *Lansing State Journal.* Lansing, Michigan; December 31, 1989.

14. Personal interview with Rev. David Brooks, December 2002.

15. Dr. Sam Hoyt. *Dedication of the Howard Sugden Chapel*. A sermon delivered at South Baptist Church, Lansing, Michigan; April 1994.

16. *Lansing State Journal*. Lansing, Michigan; December 31, 1989.

17. Personal letter from Susan Philip, March 2002.

18. Personal interview with Elmer and Pauline Sugden, August 2002.

19. *South Baptist Church Bulletin*. Lansing, Michigan; April 30, 1961.

20. Howard Sugden. *God Gives Help*. A sermon delivered at South Baptist Church, Lansing, Michigan; September 21, 1986.

21. *This Is Your Life*. Presented at South Baptist Church, Lansing, Michigan; March 1958.

22. Personal interview with Dr. Bob Shelton, September 2002.

23. *Lansing State Journal*. Lansing, Michigan; December 31, 1989.

CHAPTER 7

GREAT FRIENDS

A home-made friend wears longer than a store-bought one.
—*Ambrose Bierce*

THE apostle Paul was being taken to Rome as a prisoner. Before they arrived at their destination, the ship docked at Sidon. Paul was allowed to "go to his friends so they might provide for his needs" (Acts 27:3 NIV). Some scholars suggest that the Greek term *tous philous*, "the friends," was a common title for all Christians. Over the years, Howard had gathered around him his own *tous philous*, great friends who encouraged his heart, challenged his life, and helped shape his thinking.

H. H. SAVAGE

One of the greatest influences on Howard's life came from Dr. Henry H. Savage. Savage grew up in Colorado. His mother prayed that her son would enter the ministry, but Henry had other plans. He graduated from the University of Colorado with a Master's degree in Engineering. It was while Henry was in Boulder that Billy Sunday held special meetings there and Henry came under deep conviction of his sin and his need for Christ. A few weeks later, while attending a Bible study class, he trusted Christ as his Savior. He attended Moody Bible Institute for a year, specializing in music, but he had no thoughts of becoming a preacher. In 1911, a church in Barron, Wisconsin, needed a pastor and asked Moody for a recommendation. Even though he was not a ministerial student, they sent Henry. He stayed to become the permanent pastor of the church. Not only did he shepherd that small congregation, he married the church organist, Bessie Jenson. He pastored a second church in Wisconsin before coming to the First Baptist Church of Pontiac, Michigan, in 1924. That ministry lasted thirty-eight years![1] Henry Savage had no formal Bible or theological training but accumulated a large library of over 3,000 volumes and became a serious Bible student.

Howard first heard this bold preacher over the airwaves of eastern Michigan, and was encouraged to become a preacher himself. There are many similarities between Howard and Henry. Both were self-made scholars with large libraries; both would enjoy long pastorates lasting over thirty-five years; both men were recognized as the preeminent leaders among Baptists in the state during their day; and both maintained radio broadcasts throughout their ministries. In many ways Henry Savage laid down the pattern for ministry that Howard followed.

Dr. Savage is also known for the founding of the Maranatha Bible Conference near Muskegon, Michigan. When Savage purchased the property for Maranatha from the Paul Rader Evangelistic Association in 1936, Howard accompanied him, giving encouragement. Throughout the years, Howard was a featured speaker at this summer conference, and was present when, in 1943, a skinny young student from Wheaton College gave one of his first public sermons along the banks of the Mona Lake canal; his name—Billy Graham.[2]

Wherever Howard pastored, he always invited his trusted friend, Henry Savage, to speak. It would be extremely difficult to measure the impact that Henry had on Howard's life and ministry. Howard would not have been as effective in his ministry, humanly speaking, without the influence of Savage. When Dr. Savage died in December of 1967, Howard was there to pay tribute. Deuteronomy 13:6 describes the relationship that these two men enjoyed: "Your friend who is as your very own soul. . . ." They were, indeed, soul mates.

PAUL BECKWITH

Another influential friend in Howard's life was Paul Beckwith. At the age of seventeen, Paul toured the country with Billy Sunday, singing and playing the piano. Later he joined the Homer Rodeheaver Evangelistic Team as their pianist and secretary. After graduating from Dallas Theological Seminary in 1938, Paul was involved in an itinerant ministry of preaching, teaching, and singing, and was connected with the evangelistic work of Homer Hammontree.

Paul met Howard and Lucile during their Perry days and they immediately developed a deep friendship. He ministered with the Sugdens countless times when they were in Jackson and London. In the late 1950s, Paul moved into a home next to South Baptist in Lansing, making this residence the base of his itinerant ministry. Although he was gone throughout much of the year, Paul would minister at South Church with Howard whenever he was home.

Elaine Andrews remembers coming to South Baptist Church in 1964. She and her husband, Bob, had just moved to Lansing and were looking for a church home. They attended an evening service at South and noticed their good friend, Paul Beckwith, playing the piano. The Andrews were excited to see a friendly face. Paul spotted them during the service and hurried to them afterward. They told him the story of their desire to find a home church. Paul exclaimed, "Well, you must come to South. It's got the best preaching in town!"[3]

As Paul had formerly teamed with Sunday, Rodeheaver, and Hammontree for gospel meetings, he now joined with Howard. Whether at South Church or traveling to another city, the two made an effective team as Paul would sing and play the piano, and Howard would preach. Their philosophy of ministry was identical, and their warm personal friendship gave their ministry greater impact. The words of Mencius describe the long friendship that Howard and Paul enjoyed: "Friendship is one mind in two bodies."[4]

A WHO'S WHO IN EVANGELICALISM

Howard's friendships covered the entire twentieth century of evangelical history. From Billy Sunday to Billy Graham, he developed a good relationship with many great men of God. As a student at the Winona Lake School of Theology, Howard had his first meeting with Billy Sunday. Sunday was living at Winona Lake during the time when Howard and Lucile traveled to Indiana to further their theological training. During their first summer there, they were thrilled to spend time with the famous evangelist. Whether consciously or unconsciously, Howard developed a preaching style similar to that of Sunday's . . . theatrics included!

Billy Sunday was a man of strong faith. He took the Bible at face value and acted upon it. Lucile recalls:

Charles and Ida
Sugden with
Orie (top) and
Howard
1908

Howard, 18 years old.
This may be the very
rifle that drove
Howard to seek
the Lord
1926

High School graduation

Howard and Lucile
on their wedding day,
December 21, 1928
Lapeer, Michigan

The young pastor of Ganson Street Baptist Church
Jackson, Michigan - circa 1940

Sylvia joins
the family
1950

Central Baptist Church, London, Ontario
1951-1954

The new pastor at
South Baptist Church
1954

Maranatha
Bible
Conference
1955

South Baptist Church -
Dedication of the new auditorium
1956

Howard's degree from Wheaton College was the
first of three honorary doctorates
1956

At home in the 1960s

Howard's vast library of over 15,000 volumes was housed in four separate rooms

After 25 years of loyal service at South - 1979

Preparing to preach at a summer Bible Conference

Dr. George Sweeting welcomes Dr. Sugden as a Moody Bible Institute honorary alumnus

Howard Frederic Sugden
April 4,1907 - October 14, 1993

When we were at Winona Lake, we met Billy Sunday. That was wonderful! One time we needed rain so badly that we had a prayer meeting in the small chapel on the hill. We all met and started to pray. All of a sudden a man stood in back of me and started to pray with such zeal, that if I had an umbrella, I would have put it up right then! I looked back to see who the man was and it was Billy Sunday. Whether it was preaching or praying, he did everything with all of his heart and all of his body. I have never heard a prayer like that in all of my life.[5]

Howard Sugden was also greatly influenced by the ministry and writings of Harry Ironside. He and Lucile met Dr. Ironside during his pastorate at Moody Church. He relayed to Howard the story of God leading him to Moody Church in spite of his Brethren convictions against professional pastors. Howard had collected all of Ironside's books and relied on them heavily in his own ministry.

Howard counted it a privilege to become acquainted with the founder of the seminary they attended in Winona Lake, Dr. William Pettingill. Pettingill was something of an aristocrat, always carrying a gold-headed cane.[6] He had a deep love for the Lord and was a thoroughgoing dispensational theologian, being one of the original editors of the Scofield Reference Bible. Because of Howard's close association with friends like Savage, Ironside, and Pettingill, he had little choice but to become a dedicated dispensationalist himself.

While speaking at Canadian Keswick and Muskoka Bible Conference in Canada, Howard developed many intimate friendships with well-known evangelical leaders. One notable friend was the late Dr. John Walvoord, former president at Dallas Seminary and author of numerous books on eschatology. He and Howard became good friends. Lucile and John's wife, Geraldine, became equally close. She had a wonderful sense of humor, but Dr. Walvoord was solemn. Their oldest son, John, who was a high-school student at the time, was with his family at Canadian Keswick. He came to his dad, and said, "Why can't you be funny like Dr. Sugden?"[7] To be sure, Walvoord was a great man, even without a noticeable sense of humor. One year, Howard spoke at Dallas Seminary for graduation, and while there enjoyed the wonderful hospitality of the Walvoords.[8]

Dr. Richard Holliday, the former director of Muskoka Baptist Conference, says the list of men who spoke during the summer was a veritable Who's Who in the ministry; men like Joseph Stowell, Jr. and Joe Stowell, III, Wilbur Welch, Oswald Sanders, Earl Radmacher, J. Vernon McGee, Lehman Strauss, James and David Jeremiah, Paul Dixon, Stephen Olford, Marvin Rosenthal, Mel Johnson, Haddon Robinson, Paige Patterson, Bruce Dunn, Lee Roberson, John Whitcomb, Erwin Lutzer, and Howard Hendricks.[9] Some of these men only came to the conference because of Howard's influence. He invested many personal hours to build up these Canadian retreat centers and felt personally connected to them. He once said, "Mr. Gordon Bish, director of Canadian Keswick, was my boss for twenty-six years," simply because he spoke at Keswick for twenty-six straight summers.[10]

Howard had a bulletin board hanging over his study desk with pictures of his spiritual heroes. Some twenty-four different individuals were featured on that board—A. T. Pierson, James Grey, F. B. Meyer, A. C. Dickson, R. A. Torrey, A. C. Gaebelein, and of course Savage, Sunday, Ironside, and Morgan.[11] The connecting trait of all of these prominent men was their love for and their ability to expound the Scriptures. Some were more evangelists than expositors, but all were mightily used of God to proclaim the truths of Scripture. Hebrews 12 describes being "surrounded with a great cloud of witnesses." This was Howard's cloud, and by their silent presence, they encouraged him to faithfully serve the Lord and preach His Word.

FRIENDS AT CHURCH

Howard and Lucile were convinced that they could not have close personal friends in their own home church. To do so, they thought, would be to play favorites and promote jealousy among other members. Therefore, they were friendly to all, but close to none.

Sometimes, however, Howard would develop a special relationship with some of the children. This was true with Joyce Henry. When Joyce discovered that her birthday was on the very same day as her Pastor's, she was thrilled. Howard told her that they were "twins." Three months before their birthday, Joyce would start the countdown and remind Howard every Sunday. He always acted excited. As the day of their birthday grew near, he would ask Joyce, "How old are we going to be?" He always claimed to be the same age as Joyce. On the day of their birthday, Joyce would call Pastor and sing "Happy Birthday to us," and he would always sing back, "Happy Birthday to you." Years later, when Joyce was playing the piano for an evening service at South, Howard announced to the entire congregation that they were twins. He then told the people that they used to be the same age, but now Joyce was older.[12]

NEW FRIENDS

Making new friends was natural for Howard. One time he was preaching at a conference in Williamsburg, Virginia. Howard would do the Bible teaching and the conference leadership would find someone to do the special music. While registering at the hotel, Howard met the guest song leader—Doug Oldham. He had never seen nor heard of Doug before. Howard recalled the situation when they first met:

There was this huge man, a very, very large man. I had to hug him in sections. And the very first words that came out of his mouth to me after we met were these, "Let's eat!" I said to myself, "I'm not sure he needs that!" But away we went to have dinner together. We talked about what we'd like to see happen in the meeting, and plans were made. We came that night to the service. . . . I'd never heard him sing before on record or tape and did not quite know what to expect. I anticipated that Doug would start the service in a normal fashion by saying, "We are going to sing hymn number so-and-so." But he did not do that. When it was time for the service to begin, and with the crowd still talking, Doug walked up onto the stage. He stood at the edge of the platform and turned around to the congregation, and without any music, he began to sing "He Touched Me." I never got over that song, "He Touched Me." I began to sing it that night, then the next morning, "He touched me, oh, He touched me, and oh, the joy that floods my soul." I'm so glad that God is in the touching business.[13]

100

Doug Oldham and Howard Sugden became lifelong friends.

W.W.W.

Perhaps the greatest friend that Howard had outside of Lucile was Warren Wendell Wiersbe. Warren had heard Howard speak over the radio at Moody Founders Week in Chicago during the 1950s. However, they never met until they were conference speakers at Keswick during the same week. Warren relates the story of their first meeting:

> It was August 1963, when Betty [Warren's wife] and I made the first of many trips to Canadian Keswick. One of the blessed by-products of that visit was meeting Dr. and Mrs. Howard Sugden, who became dear friends and with whom we often traveled and ministered.[14] The first night at Keswick, our room was next door to the Sugdens. Late at night, we heard a radio broadcast. I said to Betty, "That sounds like a baseball game!" I went out of our room for something, and there was Howard in all his sartorial splendor; his hair was messed up and he was wearing a bathrobe. In the daytime, Howard's dress is immaculate, but at night he should not be seen! The radio we heard was broadcasting a baseball game. Lucile was listening to the classic voice of Ernie Harwell describe the action of her beloved Detroit Tigers.[15]

Over the years Warren and Howard became best friends. Although Howard was twenty-two years older, they were kindred souls. If it was Henry Savage who encouraged Howard

101

toward the ministry and gave him his theological base, it was Warren Wiersbe who came along as a trusted friend to broaden his horizons and deepen his life. Warren helped Howard to relax. One of Howard's associates at South Baptist said, "Warren Wiersbe gave Howard depth, and he owes a lot more to Warren than he might realize."[16]

The two pastors would call each other every week and talk about preaching and books. Warren would always call Howard the day after his birthday, "to avoid the traffic!"[17]

What a team the two of them made at Keswick. It was excellent Bible teaching with some vaudeville thrown in on the side. The one-liners came with lightning speed. They would work the question and answer time together, after a morning teaching session. Lucile played the part of the emcee, reading the questions to her husband and Warren. Being a veteran Bible teacher in her own right, she would often answer the question before it got to the men, much to the amusement of the audience. Warren recalls one session when Lucile asked and answered the first two questions without ever giving the two pastors a chance to respond. The third question had something to do with dieting and keeping your body physically fit. Lucile, then in her mid-sixties, asked the question and began to answer. She finished her comments by asking rhetorically, "Would you believe that I used to have an hour glass figure?" Speaking for the first time, Warren quickly added, "Apparently the sands of time are sinking!" The audience exploded with laughter and the session had to be delayed for several minutes before the crowd could calm down.[18]

Warren was always amazed at the energy that Howard displayed. When asked the question, "What makes Howard

Sugden tick?" Warren says, "You need to ask, 'What made him chime every hour?'"[19] Commenting on one of Howard's trips to the Holy Land, Warren said, "Howard ran today where Jesus walked!"[20]

The Wiersbes and Sugdens visited England two times together and even vacationed in Hawaii once. In Hawaii, Howard came to Warren and said, "I won't be with you this Sunday. I've found a place to preach." Richard Holliday's brother was pastoring a small church on the island. After they met, the pastor developed a sore throat and asked Howard to preach on Sunday. He was only too happy to oblige.[21]

Howard hated the water. Finally, Lucile and Betty, the swimmers of the group, lured the men into the ocean. They only waded into the water up to their knees. No one could ever remember seeing Howard Sugden in a bathing suit before. He was an unusual sight, especially wearing his glasses. Warren said, "Why are you wearing your glasses?"

Howard's response, "Because I might meet a fish."[22]

While they were traveling through Scotland, a well-meaning friend gave them some advice that proved to be frightening. Instead of traveling on the normal route, they took a short cut called the "Devil's Elbow." This narrow road, with room for only one car to pass, had a deep cliff on the side . . . the side where Howard was sitting. Warren remembers Howard either praying or singing the whole way until they safely reached their destination.[23]

On another occasion, Howard was speaking at Moody Founders Week in Chicago and Warren was pastoring the Moody Memorial Church. Because parking spaces in Chicago were hard to come by and it was an extremely cold February night, Warren said, "I'll pick you up in front of the church right after you're done speaking and take you to your hotel." As promised, Warren picked up Howard right after the service and took him to the Drake Hotel. Inadvertently, Warren stopped a short distance before the hotel and let Howard out in front of the Playboy Club. The next morning, Howard said to Warren, "Does your car always stop at the Playboy Club?"[24]

Lucile said, "I've never seen two people so much alike as Howard and Warren."[25] "In many ways, we are both 'closet introverts,'" said Warren. "When people are around, we light up, but we would rather get away from the crowds and retire to our studies, surrounded by our books."[26]

No matter how close the friendship, good friends still need their space. Richard Holliday recalls a time when both Warren and Howard were speaking at Muskoka. "You're not having Howard stay in the same room with me, are you?" Warren said to Holliday. Because of the crowd they were expecting that week, that was the plan. However, Richard said, "I'm sure we can work out an arrangement so you'll have your own spot." Warren said, "You know what the problem is? It's not that I don't enjoy being with Howard; it's just that he's like a Jewish mother! He wants to tuck me in at night, to carry my books, to make sure my shoes are polished and ready for the next day. He smothers me with so much kindness, I can't get anything done."[27]

Howard wanted Warren to follow him at South Baptist Church, but Warren was convinced it would never work out. Besides, the Lord had other plans for him: Moody Memorial Church, the Back to the Bible Broadcast, and many useful books and commentaries to write.

Warren declares that the greatest impact Howard made on him was simply their personal friendship. "I think I was the son he never had. We did so many things together. He always gave you a blessing."[28]

"I was also impressed with his consistency. He was always the same. He was always preaching or preparing to preach."[29]

"Probably the greatest lesson I learned from Howard was the importance of connecting with people," Warren commented. It was Howard's practice to walk up and down the aisles before a service and work the crowd, greeting the people in the pews. Wiersbe called this Howard's ability to "perambulate." "He truly loved people and thought the best of them. All his geese were swans!"[30]

"Although he was a man of eccentricities, and he didn't possess the gift of administration, he was truly a man of God. He had all the essential marks of a good pastor: an excellent mind, a love for people, and he was totally committed to preaching."[31]

CLOSEST FRIEND

Outside of Jesus, Lucile was Howard's best friend. Much has already been said about her. They had been partners in the work of the ministry since the Lord brought them together in 1927. "They were a matched pair," says Elaine Andrews. "He loved to preach, she loved to teach, and often they would do their study together."[32]

At Howard's retirement banquet in 1989, after sixty years in the ministry, thirty-five years at South Baptist, and sixty-one years of marriage, Howard said to his adoring congregation, with Lucile standing by his side, "*We* have had the privilege of being *pastors* of the greatest church family that could possibly be" (italics added). Howard recognized that Lucile added so much to his own personal ministry and his pastoral success. He showed tremendous deference to her, always calling her "Little Dumpling," and waiting on her hand and foot. It is nearly impossible to think of one without the other.

Ralph Waldo Emerson used to say, "The only way to have a friend is to be one." Howard was a dear friend to many, and his dear friends were a treasure to him.

And it is these dear friends who were blessed to have enjoyed Howard's most endearing characteristic of all: his humor!

END NOTES

1. *Gospel Echoes*. Published by First Baptist Church, Pontiac, Michigan; December 1961.
2. *Muskegon Chronicle*. "Billy Graham's Visit Will Recall How He First Tasted Fame Here." Muskegon, Michigan; June 1956.
3. Personal letter from Elaine Andrews, September 2002.
4. Meng-Tze (Mencius). *Chinese Classics*, Vol. 2: "The Works of Mencius." James Legge, translator. Taipei: SMC Publishing, 1998 reprint.
5. Personal interview with Lucile Sugden, November 2001.
6. Ibid.
7. Ibid.
8. Ibid.
9. Personal interview with Dr. Richard Holliday, November 2001.
10. Howard Sugden. *In Time of Change*. A sermon delivered at South Baptist Church, Lansing, Michigan; November 9, 1980.
11. Personal interview with Dr. Sam Hoyt, February 2002.
12. Personal letter from Eileen Ellis, August 2002.
13. Howard Sugden. *Look, A King*. A sermon delivered at South Baptist, Lansing, Michigan; March 27, 1988.

14. Dr. Warren W. Wiersbe. *Be Myself*. Denver: Victor Books; 1994, p. 193.

15. Personal interview with Dr. Warren Wiersbe, January 2003.

16. Personal interview with Dr. Ted Ward, August 2002.

17. Personal interview with Dr. Warren Wiersbe, January 2003.

18. Ibid.

19. Personal interview with Dr. Warren Wiersbe, February 2002.

20. Ibid.

21. Personal interview with Lucile Sugden, June 2001.

22. Ibid.

23. Personal interview with Dr. Warren Wiersbe, January 2003.

24. Ibid.

25. Personal interview with Lucile Sugden, June 2001.

26. Personal interview with Dr. Warren Wiersbe, January 2003.

27. Personal interview with Dr. Richard Holliday, November 2001.

28. Personal interview with Dr. Warren Wiersbe, January 2003.

29. Ibid.

30. Ibid.

31. Ibid.

32. Personal letter from Elaine Andrews, September 2002.

CHAPTER 8

THE LIGHTER SIDE

Being cheerful keeps you healthy.
It is slow death to be gloomy all the time.
—*Proverbs 17:22, The English Version*

IF preaching is, as Phillips Brooks suggests, "the communication of truth by man to men . . . the bringing of truth through personality,"[1] then it was physically and psychologically impossible for Howard Sugden to be anything but humorous. Humor to Howard was as natural as breathing out and breathing in. His personality was permeated with a "wonderful sense of the ridiculous. He had a contagious laugh and smile. He was filled with joy."[2]

Some would argue that humor has no place in preaching since the spiritual issues of life are too serious for any form of amusement. Others, while not denying its place, would greatly caution its use. Howard's friend, the famous British preacher Martyn Lloyd-Jones, once wrote:

> I would not dare to say that there is no place for humor in preaching; but I do suggest that it is not a very big place because of the nature of the work, and because of the character of the Truth with which we are dealing. The preacher is dealing with and concerned about souls

108

and their destiny . . . the most one can say for the place of humor is that it is only allowable if it is natural. The man who tries to be humorous is an abomination and should never be allowed to enter a pulpit.[3]

Others see the proper use of humor as an effective device in the art of preaching. Phillips Brooks observes:

Humor endows the perception of the true proportions of life. It is one of the most helpful qualities that the preacher can possess. There is no extravagance which deforms the pulpit which would not be modified and repressed, often entirely obliterated, if the minister had a true sense of humor. It has softened the bitterness of controversy a thousand times. You cannot encourage it too much.[4]

Sadly, some have encouraged it too much, but this was not the case with Howard. He had a wonderful balance of the sublime and the ridiculous.

Stuart Briscoe observes, "If the preacher has a keen sense of humor, then it would be strange if humor were not a powerful weapon in his armory."[5]

It would be strange to think of Howard without humor. His humor was both innate and deliberate, appropriate for the pulpit and out of it, even according to Lloyd-Jones' standard. In reality, it would have been easier to stop Howard from eating than from seeing the lighter side of life. He knew that humor was a mighty weapon in his preaching arsenal and he was not afraid to utilize it.

PULPIT HUMOR

Realizing that laughter can open up the mind and heart to spiritual truth, Howard gladly employed humor to disarm his hearers. In 1987, a little booklet was printed and distributed to the church family entitled, "Be of Good Cheer." It was a compilation of some pithy sayings and humorous quotations that Howard frequently used in his sermons.

Howard loved to invoke the pun. Talking about the church nursery, he said, "All our little babies are in the bawlroom, they are part of the infantry!"[6]

On another occasion, he said, "I read in the paper recently that coffee could kill you . . . Maxwell House, Good to the last drop!"[7]

"All kittens are cute . . . it's when they grow up that they become catastrophes."[8]

Even pitiful puns engaged his auditors and carried Biblical principles home to their hearts.

Howard enjoyed employing the occasional limerick, as in this example:

> *There was an old fellow from Shrew,*
> *That discovered a mouse in his stew.*
> *Said the waitress, "Don't shout*
> *And wave it about,*
> *For others will be wanting one too!"*[9]

To get his point across about the importance of marketing, Howard loved to say:

> *The codfish lays a million eggs,*
> *While the lonely hen lays one.*

But the codfish never cackles
   To tell us what she's done.
And so we shun the codfish,
   While the helpful hen we prize,
This only goes to prove the point,
   That it pays to advertise![10]

Howard was no pulpit clown. The eternal outcome of the preaching event was far too important for him to be frivolous. He understood what was at stake—the glory of God and the destiny of men and women. Yet, his natural humor could not be contained. It bubbled out of him on all occasions. Howard could easily identify with the clever response of his spiritual hero, Charles Haddon Spurgeon:

A lady complained about the humor Spurgeon used in his sermons. She was a great admirer of Mr. Spurgeon and derived great benefit from his preaching. But she felt that there was too much humor in his sermons and told him so. Spurgeon was a very humble man and he said to her, "Well, madam, you may very well be right; but if you knew the number of jokes I do not tell you, and the number of things that I refrain from saying, you would give me more credit than you are giving me."[11]

Howard would also concur with the comments of D. L. Moody who, when asked how he could laugh after preaching so seriously, replied: "If I didn't laugh, I would have a nervous breakdown. . . ."[12]

Howard's keen sense of humor carried him through the difficult and serious times of ministry when he might otherwise have fallen beneath the burden.

Howard once met a man who was antagonistic toward the church. When he found out that he was talking to a preacher, the man announced, "I won't go to church because there are too many hypocrites there." Without skipping a beat, Howard retorted, "Don't let that stop you! We can always use another one!"[13]

LIGHTHEARTED MOMENTS

Howard had a wonderful way of always finding the light-hearted side of life. As he enjoyed one of his favorite pastimes, walking through graveyards and reading headstones, he came across this interesting inscription:

Pause my friend as you go by, As you are now, so once was I,
As I am now, so you will be. Prepare my friend to follow me!

Warren Wiersbe recalls Howard's immediate response:

To follow you is not my intent . . .
Until I know which way you went!

If not original, the comeback was appropriate, and Dr. Wiersbe broke out in laughter.[14]

Howard was on his way to a meeting at the Muskoka Baptist Conference in Canada, where he was the featured speaker. He was carrying his Bible in his hand when the toe of his shoe caught the top of a step and he fell head first down a long flight of stairs, doing a complete cartwheel and a few somersaults before he reached the landing. Nearby, Dr. Richard Holliday, the director of Muskoka, heard the tremendous rumble in the stairwell and came running to see what had happened. When he arrived, Howard was sitting upright, having landed on his seat on the last step, Bible still in hand. Somewhat stunned, Howard looked up sheepishly and said, "I'm sorry to drop in on you like this . . . I was just having my devotions!"[15]

Another time, while traveling in Britain with Warren and Betty Wiersbe, the Sugdens stopped at the historic city of Truro. Their purpose was to visit the cathedral, whose beautiful stained glass windows depicted the life of Henry Martyn, one of Lucile's favorite missionaries. The Wiersbes, however, decided to stay behind and rest in their hotel room. So Howard and Lucile walked from their hotel to the cathedral. On the way, Howard, stepped in some dog manure and slipped, wrenching his back. It was a severe injury; his back immediately turning black and blue. When he relayed the story to Warren, Howard said, "Warren, when we get back home, don't tell anyone that I stepped in manure. Tell them I was hit by a Rolls-Royce!"[16]

In 1986, Howard had colon surgery, and while he was convalescing in the hospital, Warren traveled from Chicago to pay a visit. As Howard and Warren were conversing, Howard looked at Warren, and with a serious tone of voice said, "Warren, this colon surgery will destroy my preaching!"

"How is that?" Warren asked incredulously.

"All I have left is a semi-colon!"[17]

Howard was not opposed to passing on a funny story or joke that he had heard elsewhere. In one sermon, while talking about his family, Howard shared these well-known words, "My aunt gives a wonderful organ recital. After fifteen minutes in her presence, you hear about her kidneys, her bladder . . . she pulls out all the stops."[18]

Howard Sugden enjoyed a continual feast of joy as he lived life with a merry heart (Proverbs 15:15). Not only was he well fed, he fed well the congregation under his care . . . with joy!

HE LOOKED THE PART

Garrison Keillor noted, "God writes a lot of comedy . . . the trouble is, He's stuck with so many bad actors who don't know how to play funny."[19] When God created Howard Sugden, He created someone who could play funny—he even looked the part! Howard remarked to a friend, "Have you ever seen G. Campbell Morgan with that long neck and the collar he wears? He looks like a turkey coming out of a chimney!"[20] To some, Howard looked just as comical! He was quite fastidious about his clothes. He loved French cuffs, fine white shirts, and three-piece suits. He always had a handkerchief in his suit coat, folded with four points at the top. Never three, always four! His attire was always impeccable.

In the early years, Lucile had to buy his clothes from second hand sources. In later years, when he was making a better salary, he bought his clothes from one of the finer men's stores in Lansing. It was unheard of to find Howard wearing anything but a suit and tie, even while mowing the lawn!

Lucile was convinced that Howard was working too hard. She told Warren Wiersbe about the matter, and he graciously invited Howard and Lucile to fly out to Nebraska and spend several days of relaxation with him and his wife, Betty. The Sugdens agreed and were soon in the air heading toward Lincoln. The first morning after they arrived, Howard came to the breakfast table . . . dressed in a suit! Warren said, "Howard, you are on vacation! Why are you dressed like that?"

"There might be a funeral!" he answered.[21]

During a break between speaking engagements in Florida, Howard and Lucile were enjoying a few moments walking in the sand along the Gulf of Mexico. They were met by one of their church members who was attending the same conference. Gary Durow was surprised to see Howard wearing his suit and tie on the beach. He was so amused that he decided to cover a tie with cellophane and present it as a gift to his Pastor. "Now you have a tie that you can wear in the shower . . . you'll never be without one!"[22]

Howard had an unusual love affair with watches. He was known to wear four watches at the same time: two on one wrist, a third on the other wrist, and a pocket watch in his vest. When asked by a fellow pastor why he wore so many, he replied, "I don't want to be late!"[23] Others felt he wore multiple watches because they were gifts that he had received and highly valued.

Wiersbe recalls traveling through Europe with the Sugdens and noticing Howard wearing two watches.

"Why are you wearing two watches?" he inquired.

"I want to know what's happening back home!"

"That may give you the time back home, but it won't tell you the activity of those back home!"[24] Howard was not deterred. He continued to exist on his own time continuum.

To compensate for his lack of hair, Howard allowed what hair he did have to grow longer. The hair on his neck occasionally would hang over his collar, giving him the appearance of a seventeenth century Puritan, instead of a twentieth century pastor. He would comb the hair on the side of his head over the top in a vain attempt to cover some thin areas. In a strong wind, this long hair would blow about and even stand straight up on one side.[25]

A LOVABLE ECCENTRIC

Howard Sugden was eccentric. Howard's diet was always a point of curiosity. He rarely would eat beef or chicken, "I saw too many of them slaughtered on the farm and it still bothers me." But he was fond of hot dogs! Lucile loved watching the Detroit Tigers play baseball. She faithfully watched the games on television or would listen to them on the radio. Several times each season, she would venture down to the stadium to see a game in person. Howard did not want his wife to go down to Detroit alone, so he would accompany her. He had some attraction to the Tigers, but would quickly be bored with the length of the game. To make good use of his time, he would take a book. Lucile would be absorbed by the baseball game, and Howard by the book. And, of course, the hot dogs! He had to be the only fan in a stadium of 30,000 that was reading theology.[26]

Howard Sugden also loved cars; and he loved driving them fast! He used to say, "the speed limit was for everyone but pastors."[27] Dwight Bell recalls, "I think he liked to drive fast, a characteristic not uncommon to pastors, who seem to feel that the Lord's work can best be conducted at higher speeds."[28]

Living in Lansing, Michigan, the home of Oldsmobile, was the perfect place for him to indulge his affection for the auto. He would get a new car every two years. Once he was offered the keys to a brand new Cadillac as a gift from a wealthy parishioner, but he graciously declined. He believed that he should not accept a car that many people in his own congregation could not afford to drive.[29] However, Wes Youngs, a leader at South Church and owner of Youngs Trailer Sales, provided in his will that Howard be given a new sub-compact automobile. When Wes was promoted to glory, Howard received a shiny black Fiat.[30] It was quite a comical sight to see Howard blazing around the city in this tiny car. He preferred the larger cars; the Oldsmobile Cutlass being his car of choice. Many parishioners never realized that Howard enjoyed doing tight-twisting-circles with his car, doughnuts, in the fresh snow of an empty church parking lot.[31]

However, being able to navigate to a desired location was always a challenge for Howard. He once said that a map was, "nothing more than a planned way to get lost." Wiersbe adds, "If you want to talk to someone who is organized, talk to Lucile. If you want to talk to someone who is confused, talk to Howard. I'm surprised he could get out of his garage on his own."[32]

ONE MORE TIME

With the skill and timing of a vaudeville act, Howard and Lucile worked the crowds during their question and answer times at church or in Bible conferences around the country. People enjoyed listening to this loving husband and wife banter back and forth over answers to common questions that confront Christians. They offered Biblical truth with compassion and wit. The book *What Does the Bible Say About . . . ?* was compiled from their Question and Answer times at the Muskoka Conference.[33]

When Howard finally retired in December 1989, and his memory had consistently been failing him, he and Lucile rekindled the act one more time. At a dinner held in his honor, with Lucile standing by his side, he addressed the crowded banquet hall. Lucile commented, "I've always said that [your sermons] are great! If I have any criticism, I always wait until after we eat our meal on Sunday. That's the time [to give criticism]." The large audience laughed gently at her comments. Then with the timing of a veteran comedian, Howard said, "In the words of a farmer, 'You feed 'em, then you freeze 'em!'" The crowd erupted with laughter. And that familiar smile enveloped his face. He was connecting with his people once again . . . just like old times.[34]

Dr. Sugden faithfully dispensed the good medicine of a merry heart (Proverbs 17:22), and his congregation was the healthier for it.

With eternal optimism he faced every day as a beautiful day. "This is a beautiful morning; it's the forerunner of the great morning some time when Jesus will come again. It's a great day to be alive. Why, I wouldn't be dead for anything!"[35]

END NOTES

1. Phillips Brooks. *Lectures on Preaching*. New York: E. P. Dutton; 1898, p. 5.

2. Personal letter from Susan Philip, March 2002.

3. Martyn Lloyd-Jones. *Preachers and Preaching*. Grand Rapids: Zondervan; 1971, p. 241.

4. Phillips Brooks. *The Joy of Preaching*. Grand Rapids: Kregel; 1989, p. 58.

5. Stuart Briscoe. *Fresh Air In the Pulpit*. Grand Rapids: Baker; 1974, p. 173.

6. Howard Sugden. *Be Of Good Cheer*. A booklet compiled and published by Bev Shepperson: Lansing, Michigan; 1987.

7. Ibid.

8. Ibid.

9. Ibid.

10. Ibid.

11. Martyn Lloyd-Jones. *Preachers and Preaching*. Grand Rapids: Zondervan; 1971, p. 240, 241.

12. George Sweeting. *Who Said That?* Chicago: Moody; 1995, p. 247.

13. Personal interview with Lucile Sugden, June 2001.

14. Dr. Warren Wiersbe. A sermon delivered at South Baptist Church, Lansing, Michigan; June 2, 1996.

15. Personal interview with Dr. Richard Holliday, November 2001.

16. Personal interview with Dr. Warren Wiersbe, February 2002.

17. Ibid.

18. Howard Sugden. *Be Of Good Cheer*. A booklet compiled and published by Bev Shepperson: Lansing, Michigan; 1987.

19. George Sweeting. *Who Said That?* Chicago: Moody; 1995, p. 248.

20. Personal interview with Dr. Warren Wiersbe, January 2003.

21. Ibid.

22. Personal interview with Lucile Sugden, October 2001.

23. Personal interview with Dr. Sam Hoyt, February 2002.

24. Personal interview with Dr. Warren Wiersbe, February 2002.

25. Personal letter from Dwight Bell, February 2002.

26. Personal interview with Lucile Sugden, June 2001.

27. Howard Sugden. *Be Of Good Cheer*. A booklet compiled and published by Bev Shepperson: Lansing, Michigan; 1987.

28. Personal letter from Dwight Bell, February 2002.

29. Personal interview with Rev. Kenn Hecht, February 2002.

30. Personal letter from Dwight Bell, February 2002.

31. Personal interview with Rev. Don Dewey, January 2003.

32. Personal interview with Dr. Warren Wiersbe, February 2002.

33. Howard and Lucile Sugden. *What Does The Bible Say About?* Grand Rapids: Kregel; 1987.

34. Howard Sugden. *Sugden Retirement Banquet—Video.* Held at Michigan State University's Kellogg Center; December 28, 1989.

35. Howard Sugden. *Be Of Good Cheer.* A booklet compiled and published by Bev Shepperson: Lansing, Michigan; 1987.

CHAPTER 9

A MAN OF BOOKS

It is the Word of God that does the Work of God.
—Howard F. Sugden

THE driving force of Howard's life was his deep devotion to the Word of God. Paul said to Timothy, "Be diligent to present yourself approved to God as a workman who does not need to be ashamed, handling accurately the word of truth" (2 Timothy 2:15). In his desire to handle God's Word in a responsible fashion, Howard became a diligent workman, a skilled laborer in the Scriptures. He took to heart the warning of G. Campbell Morgan:

> Let me state in the briefest manner possible what I want to impress upon the mind of those who are contemplating Bible teaching, by declaring that the Bible never yields itself to indolence. Of all literature, none demands more diligent application than that of the divine library.[1]

Howard was convinced that the Bible was the inspired Word of the Living God and completely trustworthy. Therefore, he determined to study the Scriptures as hard as a farmer works his field to produce a rich feast for his family.

Normally Howard would arrive at the church before the

rest of the staff, around 6:00 a.m. He would have his private devotions for over an hour. This time was separate from his sermon preparation. Howard would take his wide-margin Bible and begin to feed his own soul, taking notes as he went. His practice was to buy a wide-margin Bible and then wear it out with study and marking. When finished with that Bible, he would place it on the shelf and purchase another one to repeat the process.[2] "That is why the Bible was written on paper, so you can take notes and write on it," Howard would often say.[3] Sometimes he would record pithy statements, maxims, sermon outlines, or cross references, in the margin of his Bible.

During his devotions, Howard loved to sing.[4] He had a decent voice and he knew the old hymns by heart. When on the platform during a worship service, he never used a hymnbook. All the hymns that were chosen he had memorized, including all the verses! His favorite hymn was Martin Luther's classic:

> *A mighty fortress is our God, a bulwark, never failing;*
> *Our helper He amid the flood of mortal ills prevailing.*
> *For still our ancient foe doth seek to work us woe—*
> *His craft and pow'r are great, and armed with cruel hate,*
> *On earth is not his equal.*
> *Did we in our own strength confide, our striving would be losing.*
> *Were not the right man on our side, the man of God's own choosing.*
> *Dost ask who that may be? Christ Jesus, it is He—*
> *Lord Sabaoth His name, from age to age the same,*
> *And He must win the battle.*

If he thought no one was nearby, he would sing to the top

of his voice. Occasionally, a staff member or custodian arrived early and, unbeknownst to Howard, took in the free concert.[5]

Howard would retreat to his house for breakfast with Lucile, briefly catch up on the daily news, then return to church for a staff meeting at 8:00 a.m. The rest of the morning Howard would devote to the study of the Word of God.

Even his detractors had to confess that Howard Sugden was preeminently a man of the Word. "I think his greatest strength probably was the fact that he knew and loved the Bible," said a co-worker who often disagreed with him. "I had great respect for him in that regard. He really loved the Bible and he valued it as an arbitrator so that decisions could be made on a basis of what we find in the Bible. He believed that and he acted upon that conviction. So his greatest strength was his adherence to and belief in the Bible."[6]

Howard used the Old Scofield Study Bible as his main text, but he was not averse to using modern paraphrases like Moffatt or Phillips. He had over forty different Bible translations that he frequently consulted in his study.[7]

While preaching, Howard would quote many different portions of scripture from memory. Lucile mentions that Howard did not have a photographic memory, but he did have a very good memory.[8] He possessed a well-disciplined mind that had been trained by frequent use. When Howard came to faith in Christ, he had an insatiable appetite for the Word of God. That hunger never waned.

On the front cover of one of his Bibles, Howard recorded his personal covenant with the Lord. It read:

Lord, I give up all my own plans and purposes, all my

own desires and hopes, and accept Thy will for my life.
I give myself, my time, my all, utterly to thee, to be
Thine forever. Fill me and seal me with Thy Holy
Spirit. Use me as Thou wilt; send me where Thou wilt;
work out Thy whole will in my life at any cost,
now and forever.
H.F.S.

Whether Howard wrote this covenant personally, or borrowed it from some other pious pilgrim, this prayer expressed his heart's desire. He wanted to know the will of God and give himself to it without qualification.

His favorite book was Hebrews, but his life verse came out of the book of Philippians, "And the peace of God, that passes all understanding, keep your hearts and minds though Christ Jesus" (4:7).[9] Most of the time he enjoyed and maintained that peace.

Howard always seemed to be studying the Word. While the Sugdens and Wiersbes were traveling in England, they arrived at their hotel late one afternoon. Of the two rooms available to them, only one had a private bath. Warren offered to give that room to the Sugdens. After settling in, Warren heard a knock on his door. It was Howard. "We have a problem! Could you please come and take a look at our room?" They went back to the Sugden suite and there Howard pointed out the difficulty. Yes, they did have a private bathroom, but the fire escape route for the entire floor came through their bathroom . . . and a sign outside of their room gave notice! "Warren, if we have a fire tonight, hundreds of people will be going through my bathroom. I don't think I can sleep knowing that!" Warren assured him that a fire was unlikely and persuaded his friend to relax. As Wiersbe was leaving the hotel room, he noticed four or five commentaries and a Bible on the bed. Howard had been in the room only a short time and was weary from travel, yet, he was studying![10]

Howard believed that God was the author of the Scriptures, and therefore, they were authoritative for all matters of doctrine, discipline, and duty. Such beliefs led him to study the Word daily and proclaim it boldly. Trying to understand Howard Sugden without taking into account his devotion to the Word of God would be to misunderstand the man entirely.

THE MAN OF MANY BOOKS

To enhance accuracy in study and fullness in preaching, Howard Sugden turned to books. When he was a student at Moody for a brief period of time, he washed windows at the Edgewater Beach Hotel—that was work! But when he and Lucile traveled to Johnson Bible College in Knoxville, he was given the job of assistant librarian—that was pure joy![11]

Howard's attraction to the printed page goes back to his childhood when his mother possessed a modest library on the family farm.[12] However, it was in 1930, during the depression era, that Howard started his personal library. It all began with a fifty-cent purchase of a cloth bound book entitled, *The Spiritual Life*.[13] Howard was thrilled with his purchase, but he knew that the money should have been used elsewhere in the modest family budget. It took him two weeks before he told Lucile what he had done. An addiction to books began to take hold. Howard would always stop at second-hand bookstores on his travels around the country, scouring the shelves of old books to find some hidden treasure.

He had no time for those who rejected the writings of men, claiming only a need for Holy Spirit instruction. Howard was convinced that the mental rubbing of his iron against the iron of the wise would do much to sharpen his knowledge. The words of Spurgeon expressed his attitude:

> Divines who have studied the Scriptures have left us great stores of holy thought which we'd do well to use. Their expositions can never be a substitute for our own meditations, but as water poured down the dry pump often sets it to work to bring up water of its own, so suggestive reading sets the mind in motion of its own account. . . . It seems odd, that certain men who talk so much of what the Holy Spirit reveals to themselves, should think so little of what He has revealed to others. . . . A respectable acquaintance with the opinions of the giants of the past, might have saved many an erratic thinker from wild interpretations and outrageous inferences.[14]

Howard started a book-purchasing practice that he continued throughout his ministry. When he would preach on a particular book of the Bible, he would call his friends at Kregel Bookstore in Grand Rapids, Michigan, and ask them to send him everything they had on that book. His neighbors became acquainted with the familiar sight of a new box of books sitting on his doorstep. Howard's library increased dramatically.

By the time the Sugdens moved to Canada, Howard had collected several thousand volumes. In 1958, his library totaled nearly 6,000 volumes. Dr. Wilbur Smith, a leading book authority, said, "Dr. Sugden's library is one of the finest private collections in the country today."[15] Lucile's perspective: "All my hats went into those books."[16]

By 1970, Howard had accumulated over 8,000 volumes;[17] in 1979, he possessed at least 9,000;[18] ten years later the number exceeded 12,000 books;[19] and Warren Wiersbe uses the ballpark figure of 20,000 volumes for the entire library.[20]

Howard's good friend H. H. Savage said, "Pastor Sugden is one of the best educated men that I know of anywhere in the use of books. He is familiar with them, he loves them, and he is able to analyze them with an efficiency that is far beyond that of the average pastor."[21]

Dr. Philip R. Newell observed: "Dr. Sugden's knowledge of the scripture through intense study, reading and meditation, is quite manifest in his ministry. There can be no doubt that one of the contributing factors involved in this is his magnificent library, which I am sure has proved to be a veritable treasure chest of blessings to his various congregations over the years."[22]

His collection was gathered from many places in the United States, Canada, and Great Britain. During the summer of 1976, the Sugdens and Wiersbes took a second trip to England. Again they met with Dr. Martyn Lloyd-Jones. After he had given them a tour around Cambridge, he took them to Heffers, one of the greatest bookstores in the world. Warren recalls: "Howard and I thought we had died and gone to heaven as we found ourselves surrounded by what appeared to be miles and miles of shelving, all crammed with books about every subject we could name."[23]

His library touched on many fields: theology, biography, archeology, philosophy, history, and contemporary themes as well, like . . . automobiles! To store his "friends," as he called them, South Church had to create an extra large office for their

Senior Pastor. Four separate rooms were dedicated to his price-less collection. His most treasured volumes were *The Complete Works of Isaac Watts*, published in 1810; *The Theology of Timothy Dwight*, published in 1838; and Benjamin Keach's book on *Metaphors of the Bible*, published in 1860. He had over fifty vol-umes of G. Campbell Morgan's works, all the writings of Joseph Parker, Charles Spurgeon, F. W. Boreham, George Morrison, and John Nelson Darby. His library included eighty sets of com-mentaries and countless research volumes.[24]

To broaden his knowledge and keep him abreast of the times, Howard subscribed to several periodicals. He read each issue of *Christianity Today*, *Time*, *Moody Monthly*, *The American Jewish Commentary*, and *The Wilson Quarterly*.

While working as a librarian at Johnson Bible College he learned the Dewey Decimal system. He adopted that topical sys-tem, with some revisions, for his own purposes. Howard always seemed to know where every book was and knew what was in every book. This seems more astounding in light of the fact that he was notorious for misplacing things. He once said, "A filing cab-inet is where you lose things alphabetically."[25] Howard never tired of his library and spent most of his waking hours there.

Rarely would Howard preach a sermon without recom-mending some book to his congregation. Often, in the evening service, he would bring a stack of books to the pulpit and men-tion their significance. After talking about them, he would let them fall to the platform with a "thud!" For a man who loved books, this seemed like rough treatment. There the books would remain in a jumbled pile until the service had concluded.[26]

Howard also wanted to encourage other pastors to give themselves to books. He often would quote the words of

Spurgeon, "If I can save a poor man from spending his money for that which is not bread, or, by directing a brother to a good book, may enable him to dig deeper into the minds of truth, I shall be well repaid."[27] When Howard would speak at pastors' conferences, he would hand out a list of recommended books. One such list, given out in 1990, was entitled, "Don't Forget the Books" (2 Timothy 4:14). The sheet contained his favorite commentaries, authors, word studies, Bible dictionaries, and sermon collections.

When the day came for Howard to retire, the books became a problem. Because he had to vacate his study, he could not leave them at the church, and his house was entirely too small to hold such a collection. His library had grown so large and he so frail that he could not get full use out of his "friends." South Church offered to build an extension onto the Sugden home to hold 3,000 volumes, but what about the others?

A call came from Dr. James Grier, dean of the Grand Rapids Baptist Seminary. They needed to increase the size of their library to meet certification standards for a new degree program the school was planning to offer. A partial donation of Howard's library would be sufficient.

Howard had a dilemma. He asked Warren, "If you could take only 3,000 books, what would you take?" "That's easy," Wiersbe replied, "You take the ones you use the most. Howard, you could throw 5,000 of your books into the Grand River and never miss them!"[28] He didn't throw them into the river. After much thought and a tearful good-bye, Howard donated 7,000 books to Grand Rapids Baptist Seminary.[29]

After Howard passed away, the rest of his books were sold to individual pastors, or to Kregel's Bookstore in Grand Rapids.

An employee at Kregel's recalls a pastor coming in from California to purchase books in December of 1993, just two months after Howard's passing. He filled a shopping cart full of used books, many of them coming from the personal library of Howard. That California pastor was Chuck Swindoll.[30]

Howard drank deep from the wells of the ancients, and his ministry was enriched because of it. He brought his heart preparation and scholarship into the pulpit, and the crowds were drawn to his preaching. So what was his preaching like?

END NOTES

1. G. Campbell Morgan. *The Study and Preaching of the English Bible.* New York: Revell; 1910, p. 74.

2. Howard Sugden. *Magic Moments.* A sermon delivered at South Baptist Church, Lansing, Michigan; September 28, 1983. In this sermon, Howard mentions that he bought a new wide-margin Bible and spent all day marking up Isaiah.

3. Howard Sugden. *This is the Life.* A sermon delivered at South Baptist Church, Lansing, Michigan; January 15, 1984.

4. Howard Sugden. *God Was There.* A delivered at South Baptist Church, Lansing, Michigan; April 29, 1984.

5. Personal interview with Rev. Don Dewey, January 2003.

6. Personal interview with Dr. Ted Ward, August 2002.

7. Personal interview with Dr. Sam Hoyt, February 2002.

8. Personal interview with Lucile Sugden, September 2001.

9. Ibid.

10. Personal interview with Dr. Warren Wiersbe, January 2003.

11. Personal interview with Lucile Sugden, September 2001.

12. *Lansing State Journal.* Lansing, Michigan; March 22, 1958.

13. Personal interview with Lucile Sugden, September 2001.

14. Charles Haddon Spurgeon. *Commenting on Commentaries.* London: Banner of Truth Trust; reprint of 1876 edition, 1969, p. v.

15. *Lansing State Journal.* Lansing, Michigan; March 22, 1958.

16. Personal interview with Lucile Sugden, June 2001.

17. *These Forty Years.* Published by South Baptist Church, Lansing, Michigan; November 1970.

18. *Twenty-Five Years of Loyal Service.* Published by South Baptist Church, Lansing, Michigan; March 1979.

19. *A Centennial Celebration.* Published by South Baptist Church, Lansing, Michigan; April 1989.

20. Dr. Warren Wiersbe. *Be Myself.* Denver: Victor Books; p. 193.

21. *Twenty-Five Years of Loyal Service.* Published by South Baptist Church, Lansing, Michigan; March 1979.

22. Ibid.

23. Dr. Warren Wiersbe. *Be Myself.* Denver: Victor Books; p. 209.

24. *Fortieth Celebration of Howard's Ordination.* Published by South Baptist Church, Lansing, Michigan; November 1970.

25. Personal interview with Lucile Sugden, June 2001.

26. Personal letter from Jim Hunsucker, Sr., January 2003.

27. Charles Haddon Spurgeon. *Commenting on Commentaries.* London: Banner of Truth Trust; reprint of 1876 edition, 1969, p. v.

28. Personal interview with Dr. Warren Wiersbe, January 2003.

29. Personal interview with Lucile Sugden, June 2001.

30. Personal letter from Carol Patrick, February 2001.

CHAPTER 10

THE PULPIT HIS THRONE

I'm preaching this Sunday and I'm getting ready today.
—Howard F. Sugden

HOWARD was singular in his focus. "Pastoral work was adjunct to his passion for preaching. He felt that he was sinning if he wasn't preaching."[1] With the apostle Paul, Howard could say, "Woe to me if I do not preach the gospel" (1 Corinthians 9:16). From the time of his conversion to the day of his home going, Howard Sugden was consumed with a passion to preach. It was never far from his mind. It was always on his heart.

SERMON PREPARATION

In the early days of his ministry, Howard would prepare his messages with the aid of Lucile. They researched the Bible together, often laying out the Scriptures on the living room floor using discarded Bibles, which they literally disassembled. They would study for hours, discussing the text and related passages.[2]

Howard had three individual desks in his four-room study at South Baptist, and each desk had its own designated purpose. One was reserved for his Sunday morning sermon; the second was dedicated to his Sunday night message; and the third was used for preparing the Wednesday night study. Each desk was covered with the books, taken from his library, that he intended to use for that particular message.

Howard would write out his sermons in longhand. Then he would take a sheet of 8½ x 11 inch onionskin paper and fold it in half. The folded paper enabled him to secure his notes to his Bible with the aid of a rubber band. Using the "hunt-and-peck" technique, Howard would type his notes, single-spaced, on only one half, of one side of the paper. If he needed more than one side, he would use another sheet and fold it as before. Lucile had been a typewriting teacher for many years, but Howard refused to let her teach him how to type. He preferred his proven method.[3] He used colored markers to highlight important points in his sermon notes.

For the Sunday evening service, Howard would have his secretary, Doris Seger, type out the full outline of his message on a sheet of 8½ by 11 inch paper. The outline would be distributed to the congregation at the conclusion of the service.

Howard once told a group of preachers that he normally spent fifteen hours a week on a Sunday morning sermon, ten hours on a Sunday evening message, and several hours for a Wednesday night study.[4] He also had the responsibility of teaching a weekly Sunday School class between his two Sunday morning services.[5] Because of the informality of the class and an extended question and answer time at the end of every session, the need for preparation was minimal. Each week Howard was preparing and teaching four messages, not to mention the sermons he would deliver as a visiting speaker in area churches or pastors' conferences.

"Preaching never gets any easier. It is always hard work because the bar gets higher. You cannot let up! It is easy to get lazy in the ministry."[6]

During his sermon preparation, Howard would pace around his study preaching to his books. Even though he was a naturally gifted and skilled orator, he worked very hard at perfecting his craft.[7]

PREACHING WITH STYLE

Howard was full of energy. Whatever he did, he did with all his heart, and this included preaching. He introduced his sermon on February 20, 1983, by saying: "My doctor just said to me a moment ago, 'There are two things you ought not to do this morning while preaching: One is to walk, and the other is to yell.' I said to him, 'You just stopped my preaching!'"[8]

"Something in his constitution rendered him unable to stand in one place. . . . He was the quintessential peripatetic preacher. [He] not only compels you to listen to what he says, but also to watch what he does. [You] don't want to miss anything."[9]

While preaching at Moody Founders Week on "Elisha, The Bald-Headed Prophet," Howard became Elisha! He not only described the action, he demonstrated it, walking back and forth across the stage, showing how Elisha rebuked the mocking youths and how forty-two of them were mauled by bears. The students were spellbound.[10]

In his own church, Howard was all over the platform. To drive a point home, he would stand on the communion table with one foot and strike a prophetic pose in typical Billy Sunday fashion. On occasion, he would sit on the organ and converse with the congregation. He would climb the pulpit, causing many to fear he would fall at any moment.[11] These theatrics did keep everyone awake!

One of the side attractions of every Sugden sermon was his battle with the microphone cord. The church sound technician supplied an extra long cord for Howard, but he often would exceed the cord's limit and be jerked suddenly to a halt. The cord became tangled and he would struggle to straighten it out to escape its grasp, while never missing a beat in his sermon. At times, a little quick step was needed to recover his balance.[12]

Frequently he would ask rhetorical questions of the audience and draw them in by talking to specific individuals. When discussing England, he might turn around and have a brief chat with Em Chapman, a choir member who came from that country. After he had finished, he would turn back to the congregation and resume his message.[13]

Howard's staff was required to sit on the platform in massive wooden chairs during the morning service. After making a point in his message, he commonly would turn around and say to a staff-member like Ted Ward, "Isn't that right, Dr. Ward?" Woe to the pastor who wasn't paying attention![14]

The thought of being dull or dry as a preacher was repulsive to Howard. He said, "There are some preachers that are so bad, the oil-well diggers ought to hire them. They are so boring." He liked to tell the story of the man who sat down in church, put his arm around his wife, and waited for the sermon to begin. Pinned to his arm was this little poem, which the people behind him could easily read:

> *Now I lay me down to sleep,*
> *The preacher's dry, the sermon's deep,*
> *If he should quit before I wake,*
> *Please give my arm a little shake.*[15]

Howard also knew how to use his voice. He would speak in conversational tones with excellent diction. At times you could detect a Canadian accent that he adopted from his brief stay in Ontario. Words like *shedual*, *aboot*, and *holiday* instead of vacation, commonly fell from his lips.[16] To emphasize a point, he would raise the volume of his voice, building up to a climax, then dramatically pausing before returning to his former tone. He often lengthened words for emphasis and effect—"Yooou are loved by Gauud."

His voice would be strong in quality, and then become soft, often breaking, giving the impression that he would soon cry. Critics felt that this was contrived.[17] Most sensed the true emotion of his soul breaking through.

PREACHING WITH SUBSTANCE

"His sermons were 'prepositional' in nature. They possessed a clear outline and moved dramatically from content-centered to intent-centered," recalled Warren Wiersbe.[18]

At the beginning of his ministry, Howard's messages were brief. During his Lansing days, his sermons were thirty-five to forty minutes long. As he grew in depth, his sermons grew in length. Once, when someone asked him, "Pastor, how long are you going to preach tonight?" He said, "A long time . . . I feel it coming on."[19]

Howard believed that preachers should take sufficient time to unfold and apply God's truth to His flock. Preaching with substance took time! He declared, "A mini-sermon is like a mini-skirt . . . it's not long enough to cover the subject!"[20]

Howard normally preached systematically through a book of the Bible on Sunday morning. On Sunday night his approach was thematic. He loved to preach on the lives of great Bible characters. Many regard his sermons on Elijah and David as his very best work.[21] Because of his love for prophecy, he decided to preach through the book of The Revelation every six years.[22]

Howard was also connected to his times. Harold Gazan, who served on the board of Deacons at South Baptist for twenty-two years, wrote in 1979:

> His sermons reflect an unusual knowledge and understanding of political events, the nuances of changes in society and culture, and a keen awareness of history, classical literature, science, philosophy, and theology. He uses current events and secular topics as a backdrop to his message; they are not the focal points. He often uses a current event, or a dramatic episode, or a biographical sketch as an opening illustration to capture the attention of his audience.[23]

Howard would talk about Abraham driving across the desert in his Oldsmobile, or one of the prophets dining at McDonalds. The young people enjoyed these comments. His message was direct and simple, with a touch of humor. Although his vocabulary was large, he did not speak to impress. "Words that are more than twelve cylinders bother me," he would say.[24]

The Greatness of God was a dominant theme in Howard's preaching.[25] "I don't want a God I can understand, I want a God bigger than that. . . . When our vision of God is small, the bigger our problems become."[26]

"My work is wholly constructive," G. Campbell Morgan

wrote in 1923, "and I believe that that is the only kind that is really of value."[27] Howard exemplified that philosophy. He was an eternal optimist. The aim of his preaching was positive and he loved to encourage the people of God. "We value things according to what we pay for them. We must be very valuable to God because He paid for us with the life of His Son."[28] "The greatest word in the vocabulary of a Christian is the word forgiveness."[29]

Howard appreciated good literature. Long sections of classical works like Shakespeare, or Milton's poetry, would be quoted from memory. He had a group of favorite poems that he used many times. Most of the faithful at South could quote these words right along with Howard:

> *Right forever on the scaffold,*
> *Wrong forever on the throne.*
> *And the scaffold sways the future,*
> *But beneath the dim unknown,*
> *Standeth God within the shadows*
> *Keeping watch above His own.*[30]

EVENINGS AT SOUTH

Although he put more time into his Sunday morning message, Howard put more advertising into his evening message. He believed that one of the best ways to build the church was to create an attractive evening service. He viewed the service as a bridge to the non-Christian world. While the morning service was not advertised in the local newspaper, the evening service was. Its title was prominently displayed on the church sign while only the morning service times were posted. The fact that non-Christians, or individuals from liberal religious backgrounds, would congregate in the evening service motivated Howard to prepare and preach clear gospel messages for these nights.

He once said that being in a church service was the greatest enjoyment of his life.[31] At his retirement banquet, December 1989, he said to the congregation, "You've always been an encouragement to me. Sometimes when I gave an awful sermon, you've come to me and said, 'Pastor, that was good.'" After Howard paused for the laughter, he added these words, "The Lord forgives lies!"[32]

GRAND RAPIDS

Howard spoke at many conferences and churches throughout the year. He was a keynote speaker at the inaugural Bible conference at the Grand Rapids Baptist College and Seminary (now called Cornerstone University) in 1959. Howard became a great draw. The students loved his antics and were blessed by his sermons. Veteran pastors and missionaries would gather to hear his positive expositional preaching. Being a favorite, Howard returned to the conference many times over a thirty-year period, delivering more than seventy messages. During the years he partnered with men like Dr. Walter Wilson, Dr. M. R. DeHaan, and R. G. Lee, to name a few. It was his love for the institution that motivated South Baptist to establish the Howard F. Sugden Scholarship for Expository Preaching at the seminary.[33]

CANADIAN KESWICK

"Keswick was the most beautiful place that I had ever seen," Lucile recalls.[34] Howard first spoke at Canadian Keswick in the summer of 1949. For twenty-seven straight summers Howard and Lucile made the journey to Lake Rosseau in Port Carling, Ontario. For twenty-two years, Howard served as a member of the Board of Directors.

The conference was interdenominational. Anglicans, United Church of Canada, Salvation Army, Methodists, Presbyterians, Baptists, and many more, all gathered to study the Word. The people loved Howard and Lucile and the love was reciprocated. They usually spent the first two weeks of August at the conference, and many from their Lansing congregation would travel the distance to be with them. Howard would also reunite with members of his previous congregations from Perry, Jackson, and London. It was the highlight of his year!

Howard would be involved in the entire schedule. He could be found helping people with their luggage, cheering on a softball team at the ball diamond, or sitting on Inspiration Point enjoying God's beautiful creation.

But preaching was his primary concern. Each morning, in the main meetinghouse, called the Delectable Mansion, with its lakefront windows providing a gorgeous view, Howard would open up the Word of God to hungry hearts. After the devotional time, he would preach again.

He loved to lead the singing as well. "You've never seen him at his best unless you've seen him at Keswick, where he was totally in charge," said Warren Wiersbe. He would take the old Sankey songbook and lead the people in worship:

'Twas Jesus my Savior who died on the tree
And purchased salvation for sinners like me.

His blood is that fountain which pardon bestows
And cleanses the foulest wherever it goes.

Howard would be walking up and down the front and singing:

And the Lion of Judah shall break every chain
And give us the victory again and again.[35]

Howard's ministry extended beyond the scheduled meetings. One time while walking down by the lake, he noticed a man sitting alone. He did not know this at the time, but the man was a surgeon from British Columbia. Howard decided to stop and strike up a conversation. "I suppose since you are here at Keswick you are a believer in Jesus," Howard observed. Without batting an eye, the man said, "No, I am not." In a few moments, Howard led the man to a saving knowledge of Christ.[36]

Unfortunately, the popular conference ran into difficult times and failed to open for the 1976 season. The buildings and grounds were sold to a corporation that failed in its attempts to make the location a nightclub and gambling establishment.[37]

Years later, Howard had a friend drive him by the camp. The place was boarded up and vacant. He said, "Take me home. I never want to see this place again." Howard was heartbroken.[38]

MUSKOKA

In 1972, before Keswick closed, Howard spoke for the first time at the Muskoka Baptist Conference just thirty miles away. Gradually, his attachment to Keswick shifted to Muskoka.

Howard became both conference speaker and host. For seventeen years the Sugdens did much to establish Muskoka as one of the premier Bible conferences in the Midwest and probably all of Canada.[39]

He endeared himself to the older congregation by calling them "kids." The young people loved his humor and stories. Even his grandson, Daniel, when he was only twelve years old, decided not to go to the children's meetings during the week. He wanted to hear Grandpa. He said, "Grandma, I love to hear him preach, because he says something funny sometimes and then he gets serious and his funny stuff helps me understand the serious stuff!"[40]

Muskoka director, Richard Holliday, states: "The Sugdens were the most popular speakers at Muskoka. Large crowds always attended their meetings and many lives were touched, including decisions for salvation. We know of no others more capable in the pulpit or exemplary of Christ-likeness than the Sugdens."[41]

In later years, a Sugden Suite was dedicated at Muskoka and still exists today. It wasn't a large apartment, but it was homey. It had a nice living room with a small fireplace. The patio had a beautiful view of the lake. The suite was theirs to use while they ministered during the 1980s.

DR. SUGDEN

Howard's preaching was appreciated all over the country. "His conference ministry is still legendary," said one pastor.[42] In honor of his effectiveness and ability, he received three honorary doctorates. The first, already mentioned, came from Wheaton College in August 1956, with Dr. V. Raymond Edmund, college president, conferring the degree. In 1971, Dr. Earl Radmacher conferred upon Howard an honorary doctorate from Western Conservative Baptist Theological Seminary in Portland, Oregon. Dr. Wilbur Welch gave Howard his third honorary doctorate from the Grand Rapids Baptist College and Seminary in May of 1983.

A MAN GOD USED

In December of 1979, *Time* magazine featured an article entitled "American Preaching: A Dying Art?" The editors of *Time* wrote about seven preachers who "are splendid practitioners of the ancient art of preaching." Harold Gazan, believing that his pastor was equally, if not more, deserving of recognition, followed the pattern of the *Time* article and wrote the following tribute:

> While not a large man, his presence fills the pulpit, as few men are able to do. He has a voice that invites listening, a manner that wins admiration, and a message that grips and holds the attention of his audience. He is both dignified and kinetic in his style. . . . Dr. Sugden firmly believes that the purpose of preaching is to declare the Word of God. He says, "It is the Word of God that does the Work of God." The foundation of each sermon is a selected passage from the Bible. His sermons, while exegetical, reflect an uncommon grasp of all of Scripture. The various books of the Bible are woven together in patterns of meaningful insight, and form the basis for his preaching and teaching. . . . The use of alliteration, the use of clearly stated points, humor, and his

dramatic eloquence, enabled the listener to follow the message and to identify with its content. He stimulates an interest on the part of his congregation to become personally involved in the study of the Word of God. He preaches with authority and encourages his listeners to meet the challenge of committed Christian living in a fear-filled and frustrated world.[43]

Dr. Edward Hayes, former president of Denver Seminary, called Howard "the last great orator in this country."[44] Howard's good friend Warren Wiersbe adds, "Howard was a mighty preacher of the Word."[45] He was never more alive than when he was preaching to a crowd of people the eternal truths of God's Word. Perhaps that is why God made him a shepherd to shepherds.

END NOTES

1. Personal interview with Dr. Warren Wiersbe, January 2003.
2. Personal letter from Dr. Harold Lambert, March 2002. Dr. Lambert was the Sugden family physician in Canada. He stayed in the Sugden's home for a brief time in 1963.
3. Personal interview with Lucile Sugden, November 2001.
4. Dr. Richard C. Weeks. *Pastoral Theology*. (www.hismajestysservice.org), October 2002.
5. In 1970, South Baptist started a second morning service at 8:30 a.m. in the smaller chapel. Howard preached the same message in both the 8:30 a.m. and the 11:00 a.m. services.
6. Personal interview with Dr. Sam Hoyt, February 2002.
7. Personal letter from Rev. Desmond Bell, February 2002.
8. Howard Sugden. *Have You Heard the Good News?* A sermon deliv-

ered at South Baptist Church, Lansing, Michigan; February 20, 1983.

9. Personal letter from Jim Hunsucker, Sr., January 2003.

10. Personal conversation with Rev. Kenn Hecht, October 2002.

11. Personal interview with Virginia Wood, February 2003.

12. Personal letter from Jim Hunsucker, Sr., January 2003.

13. Personal letter from Eileen Ellis, August 2002.

14. Personal interview with Dr. Ted Ward, August 2002.

15. Howard Sugden. *Be Of Good Cheer*. A booklet compiled and published by Bev Shepperson: Lansing, Michigan; 1987.

16. Personal letter from Elaine Andrews, September 2002.

17. Personal interview with Dr. Ted Ward, August 2002.

18. Personal conversation with Dr. Warren Wiersbe, January 2003.

19. Howard Sugden. *Why Pyramids Watch*. A sermon delivered at South Baptist Church, Lansing, Michigan; October 23, 1983.

20. Howard Sugden. *Be Of Good Cheer*. A booklet compiled and published by Bev Shepperson: Lansing, Michigan; 1987.

21. Personal letter from Elaine Andrews, September 2002.

22. Personal interview with Dr. Warren Wiersbe, January 2003.

23. Personal Tribute written by Harold Gazan, December 30, 1979.

24. Howard Sugden. *Be Of Good Cheer*. A booklet compiled and published by Bev Shepperson: Lansing, Michigan; 1987.

25. Dr. Sam Hoyt. *The Dedication of the Sugden Chapel*. A sermon delivered at South Baptist Church, Lansing, Michigan; April 1994.

26. Personal letter from Jim Hunsucker, Sr., January 2003.

27. Dr. Warren Wiersbe. *Walking with the Giants*. Grand Rapids: Baker; 1976, p. 135.

28. Personal letter from Jim Hunsucker, Sr., January 2003.

29. Howard Sugden. *God Has the Answers*. A sermon delivered at South Baptist Church, Lansing, Michigan; August 24, 1986.

30. Personal letter from Mae Clarkin, February 2002.

31. Howard Sugden. *Desire of the Heart.* A sermon delivered at South Baptist Church, Lansing, Michigan; February 19, 1984.

32. Howard Sugden. *Sugden Retirement Banquet-Video.* Held at Michigan State University's Kellogg Center; December 28, 1989.

33. *South Baptist Church Bulletin.* Lansing, Michigan; November 9, 1980.

34. Personal interview with Lucile Sugden, September 2001.

35. Dr. Warren Wiersbe. *Funeral Service for Howard Sugden.* A sermon delivered at South Baptist Church, Lansing, Michigan; October 1993.

36. Howard Sugden. *The Prayer of Paul.* A sermon delivered at Canadian Keswick, Port Carling, Ontario; August 4, 1965.

37. Personal letter from Dwight Bell, February 2002.

38. Personal interview with Dr. Richard Holliday, November 2001.

39. Personal letter from Rev. Desmond Bell, February 2002.

40. Personal interview with Lucile Sugden, November 2001.

41. Personal letter from Dr. Richard Holliday, August 22, 1980.

42. Dr. Robert G. Delnay. *Resources For Preaching.* (www.faith.edu/pulpits), February 2003.

43. Personal letter from Harold Gazan, December 1979.

44. Personal interview with Rev. David Brooks, November 2002.

45. Dr. Warren Wiersbe. *Be Myself.* Denver: Victor; 1994, p. 193.

CHAPTER 11

A PASTOR TO PASTORS

Your pastor has often been my pastor.
—*Warren W. Wiersbe,*
to the South Baptist Church congregation

HOWARD Sugden was serious about the task of being a shepherd. He liked to quote the *Canterbury Tales* where Chaucer gave a portrait of the country parson. He chose to call him a shepherd.

> *He dwelt at home with watchful care to keep*
> *From prowling wolves his well-protected sheep.*
> *Though holy in himself, and virtuous,*
> *He still to sinful men was piteous,*
> *Not sparing of his speech in vain conceit,*
> *But in his teaching comely and discreet,*
> *To draw his flock to heaven with noble art,*
> *By good example, was his holy art.*

"To draw his flock to heaven," Howard mused, "What an awesome task for the man with the staff in his hand and the sheep in his heart."[1]

Howard was a shepherd with great faith in God and great love for His flock. He pursued both with enormous energy.

When asked, "How did you arrive at your current philosophy of ministry?" pastor Glenn Blossom, a former staff member at South Baptist said, "One of the greatest influences for me was working for the man named Dr. Howard Sugden. . . . He is the pastor of a large church *who really gave himself to people*"[2] (italics added).

He was a patient man with his flock and spoke with kindness. "In all the years I knew him, I never once heard him raise his voice in anger," said his granddaughter, Cindy Blanche.[3] He very seldom showed any impatience, and when he talked with you, he gave you his undivided attention. He was excited to greet everyone, which is what he did before the service in the auditorium, between services in the Sunday School classes, and after the service at the door.

Howard committed his mornings to study, but in the afternoons, he would visit. Five days a week he would visit in hospitals, and his people loved him for it! He would run up the stairs to the highest floor, then visit his way back down. His calls were always brief, never lasting more than a few minutes. A greeting, a sympathetic ear, a verse of scripture, and a heart-felt prayer, and Howard was gone as quickly as he came, to visit someone else. Yet, the people were not offended, they were thrilled that their busy pastor took the time to see them! He once said:

> As a pastor, I have told our people repeatedly that when they are well and happy, we will not be at their door for a friendly spot of tea. But when we are needed in their extremities, at any hour of the day or night, we will be on hand. . . . A church will thrive with such a pastor, one who is sensitive to his people's needs and problems.[4]

Howard acknowledged that many have lost confidence in their ministers. The counseling sessions at Keswick, with people from other churches, confirmed this. He read an article in 1970 which revealed that the minister once stood at the top of the list among the most respected leaders in the community, but had by that time, slipped to twelfth.[5] Howard believed this loss of respect was due to the general disregard for biblical authority among clergy, their loss of personal integrity, and their lack of love for their people. He felt that pastors now viewed themselves as C.E.O.'s, not servants. "People wrapped up in themselves make very small packages," he liked to say.[6] Selfishness militates against servant-hood, and results in very poor ministers!

Howard's role as a pastor in Lansing extended beyond his own congregation. Once he was called upon to visit a man in the hospital whom he had never met. The man was near death. Howard was told the man could hear his voice although he could not speak. With that assurance, he held the man's hand and leaned forward to whisper the gospel to him. After sharing the good news of Christ, Howard summarized his talk with these four points:

> "Sir, God loved, God gave, You must believe, and then you will receive. If you understand what I've told you about Jesus and you want to accept Him, just push your cheek against my hand." The man did so, and Howard said, "That man was saved by a push!"[7]

"He epitomized for me what a pastor should be," said long-time member Harold Gazan.[8] South was truly blessed as a congregation with a pastor who fed them well and cared for them faithfully. Howard knew that the church was dear to the heart of God and he understood her role in the world, so he gave himself to the church. He also believed that the best way to get the church moving was to love them forward. He once wrote, "Happy is the flock of God that has a shepherd with a sense of direction, a pastor who has caught a vision of the program of God and the place of the local church in that program."[9] South was a happy place.

A SHEPHERD TO SHEPHERDS

Howard was known by many as a leader of pastors. Dr. Warren Wiersbe comments:

> If ever there was a pastor's pastor, it was Howard Sugden. Wise in the ways of the Lord and the secrets of the human heart, his counsel was sought by pastors who phoned him, wrote him, and even stopped at his office unannounced, all seeking encouragement and help in solving church or personal problems. It was always a delight to share a pastors' conference with Howard and hear him answer questions. His keen sense of humor kept us amused and his spiritual insights kept us amazed.[10]

Together Howard and his good friend, Warren Wiersbe, collaborated on a book entitled Confident Pastoral Leadership. This volume has been of immense value to many pastors. Howard took time out of his busy schedule to spend time with any pastor who called requesting counsel. Seldom did a week go by without a call from someone in the ministry.

A man who served as president of London Bible College in

Canada was asked to take a church pastorate in Toronto. He said, "I will not take the church until I go and spend a week with Dr. Sugden. I want to follow him and watch everything he does before I commit to taking the church." The man came and followed Howard for the entire week. He stayed in a motel but shared all of his meals with the Sugdens. He ended up taking the church in Toronto and having a wonderful ministry, in part due to the wise counsel of his friend.[11]

A pastor called from Montreal. He had been working as a missionary in Quebec for twenty-five years and had only one convert. Now all of a sudden, God had broken loose in the area. Many had come to know Christ. The Fellowship of Baptists were starting churches everywhere! Many of the new pastors were college graduates, but they had little or no seminary training. After hearing Howard at Canadian Keswick, the pastor from Montreal gave him a call. He had started an evangelical seminary in his church and asked Howard to come and teach Homiletics and Pastoral Theology. Men came from everywhere in the province. They slept on pews and on the church floor. Howard shared his love and knowledge with them and they were helped. Encouraging these "first generation churches" was a great thrill for him.[12]

Because of his love for pastors, his personal scholarship, his unique preaching prowess, and his years of experience in the ministry, Howard was a natural fit as a seminary teacher. In 1980, he spent ten weeks traveling seventy-five miles back and forth between Lansing and Grand Rapids to teach at the Grand Rapids Baptist Seminary with Dr. Warren Faber. For three decades, Howard was closely associated with this institution.[13]

Jim Jeffery was pastoring in Auburn, Indiana, and in need

of encouragement. He had heard Howard at the Grand Rapids conference and decided to give him a call. Howard took the call and spent the better part of an hour on the phone with this young shepherd. A further appointment was made to meet for lunch a short time later. Howard, with his normal positive outlook and keen wit, patiently listened and shared words of wisdom. Jim was amazed that this well-known pastor would take time for him. Twenty years after the encounter, he cannot forget Howard's kindness. Jim went on to pastor a large church in Grand Rapids and is now the president of Baptist Bible College in Clarks Summit, Pennsylvania.[14]

For many years Howard conducted a monthly breakfast meeting in Lansing for area pastors. As a general among generals, he encouraged the troops and taught the men the holy warfare of the pastorate. They always concluded with a Question and Answer time where Howard would shine. Among pastors, he was in his element.[15]

Dwight Bell said, "In truth he, no doubt, was instrumental in saving many churches and straightening out many lives that would otherwise have been ruined. I heard him say one time: 'When I speak to a pastor, I feel like I am speaking to an entire congregation.'"[16]

MINISTERS AND MUSKOKA

The Canadian conferences were designed to provide an environment for pastors to receive physical and spiritual refreshment. To accomplish this goal, a leader was needed who could minister and relate to pastors. Richard Holliday explains:

I loved to have men of God speaking at Muskoka who

exemplify the best pastoral skills, because we were drawing so many pastors at the time. We wanted the whole program of preaching to be led by men who could minister to other pastors, men that other pastors would want to hear from and sit under their ministry, so that they could go back to their churches, having been refreshed and blessed. My best example as a role model for men in the ministry, bar none, is Howard Sugden. He would shake the men and stir them up and send them out with the feeling that they had met with the Lord. In his winsome way, he would win their hearts as he greeted them before the service, before he ever preached from the pulpit. When he talked with you, many said, "I felt as though I was the only person on the earth." He added a dimension of intense warmth, love, and graciousness, with no false humility. You sensed that you heard from heaven when Howard spoke.[17]

COLLEGES AND FELLOWSHIPS

Howard continued his effective ministry to the students and alumni of the Grand Rapids Baptist College. Dr. Paul Dixon, President of Cedarville College, also appreciated Howard's input on campus. Dixon declared, "We loved to have Howard come and speak to the students at Cedarville. They love him, and that love is based on the fact that he cares for them. He would take the time to greet them before a service or sit and talk with them at the dining hall. He became one of the favorite speakers at Cedarville."[18]

Although he would rarely be gone from his own pulpit on

Sundays, other than the month of August for the Canadian conferences, Howard traveled often during the week to go wherever he could preach and encourage the saints of God.

Throughout the Midwest, regional ministerial fellowships would ask Howard to come and address them. He met countless times all over the nation with ministerial groups from the General Association of Regular Baptists, and the Conservative Baptist Association. He was not a member of either fellowship, but he was a trusted friend and leader. Since these two groups did not see eye to eye and had trouble getting along, it is astounding that Howard could be heavily involved with both groups at the same time and remain comrades of all.

After his retirement from South in 1989, Howard filled his weeks with ministry to pastors. He was the pastor emeritus at South and was preaching one Sunday a month, but he invested much of his time with other pastors.

In June of 1990, I attended a pastors' luncheon where Howard spoke. I wrote in my diary my impression of that occasion: "Attended a pastors' meeting in Stanton with Howard Sugden. A good meeting with a great man of God. He looks feeble and is repeating himself, and yet the meeting was inspiring."

Usually, Howard would have a staff member or layman from South drive him to his appointments during his last years. Harold Gazan was given the responsibility in the late spring of 1991. They were driving to the thumb area of Michigan for a meeting with area pastors. Harold was concerned about Howard's ability to speak clearly. He was demonstrating signs of dementia, forgetting what had happened only moments before. As they neared their destination, Harold's fears increased. But when Howard got up to speak to the men, the fog lifted, and he spoke clearly and eloquently for almost a half hour. God was still infusing Howard, at the age of eighty-four, with power to minister to His servants.[19]

In his career, Howard preached in pastors' conferences throughout the nation. On the west coast he ministered at Western Seminary in Portland, Oregon, and the Mount Hermon Conference in California. He preached on the east coast at the Rumney Bible Conference in New Hampshire, and Lancaster Bible College in Lancaster, Pennsylvania. In the South, he spoke at Moody Keswick in Florida and at Dallas Theological Seminary in Texas. And in his beloved north country of Canada, he spoke from Ontario to Vancouver.

Howard had a deep heart for pastors, and shepherding was in his soul. Dr. Wiersbe tells us that the first sentence of their book *Confident Pastoral Leadership* came from Howard: "God has called us to be pastors and to preach his Word, and, quite frankly, we enjoy it."[20]

But all was not easy for him. Behind the scenes he faced difficult battles.

END NOTES

1. Howard Sugden. *Person to Parson, An Open Letter for Pastors and People.* Edited by David Egner. Grand Rapids: Radio Bible Class; 1980, p.41.

2. *Journal of Pastoral Theology.* Portland: Western Seminary; Fall 2001, p. 7.

3. Personal interview with Cindy Blanche, February 2003.

4. Howard Sugden. *Person to Parson, An Open Letter for Pastors and People.* Edited by David Egner. Grand Rapids: Radio Bible Class; 1980, p. 45, 48, and 49.

5. *Lansing State Journal*. Lansing, Michigan; November 7, 1970.

6. Personal letter from Caroll Roost, November 2002.

7. Howard Sugden. *This is Life*. A sermon delivered at South Baptist Church, Lansing, Michigan; October 11, 1987.

8. Personal letter from Harold Gazan, June 2002.

9. Howard Sugden. *Person to Parson, An Open Letter for Pastors and People*. Edited by David Egner. Grand Rapids: Radio Bible Class; 1980, p. 46.

10. Dr. Warren Wiersbe. *Be Myself*. Denver: Victor; 1994, p. 193.

11. Personal interview with Lucile Sugden, October 2001.

12. Ibid.

13. Howard Sugden. *A Time for Change*. A sermon delivered at South Baptist Church, Lansing, Michigan; November 9, 1980.

14. Personal interview with Rev. Jim Jeffery, August 2002.

15. Personal letter from Rev. Lewis Wood, March 2002.

16. Personal letter from Dwight Bell, February 2002.

17. Personal interview with Dr. Richard Holliday, November 2001.

18. Dr. Paul Dixon. *A Lecture on Leadership*. A seminar delivered at Highland Park Baptist Church, Southfield, Michigan; May 1995.

19. Personal interview with Harold Gazan, November 2002.

20. Howard Sugden and Warren Wiersbe. *Confident Pastoral Leadership*. Grand Rapids: Baker; p. 11.

CHAPTER 12

UNSEEN BATTLES

"And it came to pass . . ."
Thank God when trouble comes,
it does not come to stay, "it came to pass."
—*Howard F. Sugden*

ALL believers face battles. At times they face external opposition. Often they struggle with internal weaknesses. Some battles are physical while others are spiritual. Some are played out in the public arena, but many are fought in the shadows of privacy. No one veiled in human flesh is exempt. Valuable lessons are learned from those who overcome obstacles and admiration is due those who, while flawed, labor valiantly on.

INSECURITY

Howard's strengths were abundantly clear—he was a man who loved God and followed His Word, a gifted preacher with a consuming love for people. Because of these gifts, he was used of God to minister to the church throughout North America. His weaknesses were more difficult to detect.

From his earliest days, Howard fought with feelings of insecurity. "Was he insecure? Oh, definitely!" remarked Dr. Warren Wiersbe, "but I'm not sure why. Perhaps he was afraid to fail."[1] Dr. Ted Ward, an associate for many years, acknowledged this fear of failure: "Howard was very concerned about the problem of the revolving door—people coming in and just as quickly going out."[2]

Another associate, Dr. Sam Hoyt, remembers Howard's concern over the migration of members from South Baptist to a sister church across town. "Why would they leave us?" Howard would lament.[3] Certainly, the fear of losing people makes most pastors feel insecure.

Some felt the feeling of insecurity was evident in Howard's need to be in charge. Harold Gazan, the longtime chairman of the deacon board, admitted that the pastor he dearly loved battled with insecurities and needed to be in control.[4] There were few functions that took place at South without Howard's participation. From social activities to worship services, he was always front and center. Some believe his involvement was dedication to the Lord; others attribute it to insecurity.

Dr. Ward said, "I admired him in many ways and felt I worked well with him. But he was insecure, and he did not know he was insecure. Many people who feel inadequate will acknowledge that sense of insecurity, but he did not know it. His way of solving things was to push himself forward, never to rest, never to recede, always driving forward. And the more uncomfortable he felt, the more active he became. He was uncomfortable, no matter what it was, unless he was running the event. I would say that was his greatest problem."[5]

While Howard appreciated great preaching, some felt he was insecure around great preachers. "He felt threatened by them," said Dr. Hoyt.[6] "He had difficulty giving up his pulpit on Sundays. He was very defensive about his space and his time in the Sunday pulpit," Dr. Ward recalled. On the rare occasions when he was gone, he was accused by some of bringing in less than effective preachers to take his place.[7]

Howard was loved by his Lansing congregation and had completed almost twenty-five years of successful ministry when he expressed a fear that few thought he would face—the fear of being fired. In the late 1970s, Howard confided to his colleague, Dr. Hoyt: "I don't know if the board will let me stay. I don't know how long they will let me be pastor."[8]

STAFF ISSUES

Howard also struggled with administration. Harold Gazan recalls: "His strengths were in the area of preaching and being a pastor. In my experience his weaknesses were in the area of administration. He was a very able leader in articulating vision for a building program or teaching pastors how to preach. He had a great need to be needed and this sometimes interfered with programs and ministry."[9] Warren Wiersbe adds, "Howard did not have the gift of administration. I told him, 'Pay attention to your wife. Our wives can really help us.' If he would have listened to Lucile, he would have been fine."[10]

This difficulty with administration was evident in his handling of the staff. He would meet with them briefly each morning for coffee and toast or doughnuts, but little work was accomplished. He had difficulty leading them to effective ministry and saw no need for strategic planning. Because they were pastors, he felt they should know what to do.

Howard was not willing or able to delegate responsibilities to staff. He saw their weaknesses and not their strengths. To his credit, he never publicly acknowledged their deficiencies, as he saw them, yet his weekly call to Warren Wiersbe often focused on his discouragement with the staff. "Warren, what am I going to do with this staff member? How can I get rid of him?"[11]

One time Warren and Howard were listening to a report from the director of a mission working with Native Americans in Arizona. Due to the unrest among the Native American population in the 1970s, this mission had lost sixty staff members in one day! While this missionary was explaining the situation, Howard leaned over to Warren and said, "How does he do it?"[12]

Ironically, while he spent time with visiting pastors, he did not invest much time with his staff as a mentor or team leader. "At times, he would undermine new ideas, although very subtly, and shine the light away from modern methods," Harold Gazan remembers.[13] Tension on the staff, while not constant, was not foreign.

Howard told his staff that he did not expect them to keep up with him. On the other hand, he could be critical of them when they did not. Howard worked on Saturdays and it disturbed him when his staff did not. Warren Wiersbe helped temper this imbalance. He reminded Howard that these men had families to care for and could not work every day of the week.[14]

"Howard Sugden had difficulty confronting a staff member," Dr. Hoyt relates. "He hated details but had difficulty delegating things to others. In a staff meeting, he would have you in stitches, but little planning was done. He'd talk about great men of God that he had rubbed shoulders with, but he never wanted to confront a staff member."[15]

Difficult issues of the church were dealt with through a liaison. Harold Gazan was often given the responsibility of handling delicate parishioner issues or staff problems on Howard's behalf.[16]

Some would say that Howard's problem with his associates began with improper selection. Associates were sometimes chosen to fill a vacant position without a thorough interview process. Many who served at South served well in spite of this deficient approach. Some did not. "It is my opinion that Pastor was not a great judge of men when it came to choosing associate pastors for the church," recalls Dwight Bell. One incident regarded a Christian Education Director.

> After an abrupt hiring process and a short ministry, tension surfaced between Pastor and the new associate. This all came to a head one memorable night when the combined deacons and trustees were gathered in the corner of the auditorium of the church, while this associate was sequestered in an office somewhere in the building. There were on-going negotiations regarding the details of his severance package, with a messenger carrying the reports back and forth. The board, as a whole, never saw the associate that night, nor did it ever see or hear from him again. I still think that night was not one of South's shining moments.[17]

A MAN OF HIS TIMES

Howard was a man of his times. Unfortunately, that included some negative baggage. "Occasionally, during the message, he would tell a joke or story making a minority person the butt of uncomplimentary humor. . . . Such remarks were, at best, culturally insensitive."[18]

For a man who truly loved people, this appeared to be a gen-

erational oversight. Howard did show signs of change. Jim
Hunsucker, a board member at South, explains:

> I recall one incident when Howard displayed the rare sort
> of deep character that enables a person to admit publicly
> to a fault or alter his behavior. Pastor mentioned to the
> deacons that he was concerned about a certain black
> male teenager who was showing interest in a white
> female. The parents of the female were concerned and
> shared their concern with Pastor Sugden. He viewed the
> boy's behavior as a problem. "Is anyone viewing the boy's
> behavior as improper?" asked a deacon.
>
> "No, nothing like that," responded Howard.
>
> "If this were a white boy showing the same attention
> to a white girl, would there be a problem?"
>
> "No, probably not," Howard acknowledged.
>
> "Do you believe, as some Christians do, that the
> Bible teaches against interracial marriage?"
>
> "Yes, I do," said Howard.
>
> "Where does it teach that?" asked the deacon.
>
> "I can show you," Howard replied, "but we don't
> have time now."
>
> The deacons quickly moved on to other business.
>
> Several weeks later, while answering questions in his
> Bible class, Howard said publicly:
>
>> Sometimes a person has to admit he has been
>> wrong in his thinking. Recently, a gentleman asked
>> me the question about interracial marriage. I
>> thought I knew the answer, but I decided to study
>> the Bible to know why I believed it was wrong. I

now can tell you that there is nothing in the Bible that can reasonably be understood to teach that we should be opposed to interracial marriage. We must be careful how we apply God's word. We should never invoke it to reinforce or justify our wrong thinking or behavior. Next question?

Howard Sugden did not believe in dwelling on contentious matters, but his change of heart showed tremendous character.[19]

OVERLY GRACIOUS

Howard was a gracious man—to a fault! He saw himself as a servant to all, but a virtue out of balance becomes a vice. He had difficulty saying "No" to anyone. Rebuking an individual, even when warranted, was excruciating.

One time at Keswick, Howard was leading a testimony service when a woman stood up to speak. She spoke for more than twenty minutes, leaving little time for anyone else. Lucile came up to Howard afterward and said, "Why didn't you stop her?" Howard replied, "I thought she might have something to say."[20]

Warren Wiersbe tells of the time when a woman asked to be baptized by trine-immersion, so as not to offend her family. Howard willingly complied, but did not disclose the fact that he had no idea how to do trine-immersion. "Howard almost drowned the lady, as he did not give her time to breathe between the three dips."[21]

Howard practiced the philosophy that most problems in life would take care of themselves if left alone. "Don't poke skunks!" he would caution.[22]

Out of a tender heart, Howard could not bring himself to

carry out church discipline. He even had difficulty disciplining his own daughter, Sylvia.[23]

THERE IS NO PROBLEM

One early morning, an associate came to the church and found Howard draped over his car in the parking lot. "Are you all right?" he asked. Howard said, "Will you help me to get to my study." The associate recognized that Howard was sick. "You don't look good; I think you should go home." Howard said again, "Please, help me to my study!" Trying a third time to encourage his pastor to return home, the associate said, "Does Lucile know that you are sick?" Howard, uncharacteristically, raised his voice: "JUST GET ME TO MY STUDY!" He stayed in his study the whole morning. No one saw him or heard from him. Although he was not functioning well, he was at work, and that was important to him![24]

Late one Saturday night, Howard fell down a flight of stairs and was taken to the hospital. He spent most of the night in the emergency room. Early Sunday morning he was at church, weak but ready to work. After preaching in the second service, he asked one of his associates to help him back to his study. "I think I'm bleeding," Howard declared. His associate pastor helped him off with his suit coat and found his white dress shirt soaked with blood! Several doctors in the church were summoned to Howard's aid. They patched him up and took him home to rest . . . so he could return for the Sunday evening service![25]

IT'S HARD TO CHANGE

Howard was an innovative pastor in the early 1950s, but his

ministry did not change in philosophy or methodology for over thirty-five years. "He was not a change agent," Dr. Ted Ward said. "He didn't know how to lead people into change. He had no capacity to provide that cutting edge toward change. He was his own worst enemy because he was so slow to change."[26]

When, in 1970, some contemporary music was presented at a Sunday evening service, voices of protest were heard. People felt that the church might be drifting from its conservative taste in music. Howard responded with what he believed was the majority view of the church:

> We live in strange days. Days when there seems to be a feeling of hopelessness and futility in life, and these feelings have crept into the music of the day. Knowingly or unknowingly, the world has made a tremendous impact upon music, and I am amazed to hear of men who were once strong who have capitulated to the new mode and mood. When we bring in our new music leader, before he assumes his position, we are going to sit down with him and make clear what we expect in the way of music as we attempt to do God's work in God's way.[27]

Howard faced some opposition to his preaching as well. Some believed his oratorical style was out of date, his "gravy had become grease." Critics called him a showman and pulpiteer. Howard once preached at a church in West Virginia. The following week the pastor was having lunch with a businessman from his congregation. The man was not in attendance on the Sunday Howard preached, but heard Howard's sermon broadcast over the radio. "Who was that guy who spoke last Sunday?"

the man asked. "That was Dr. Howard Sugden from Lansing, Michigan." The businessman scoffed, "He's nothing but a ham actor."[28]

There was a man in Howard's own church who criticized his preaching regularly. After every Sunday sermon he would tell Howard what a lousy job he had done. In time, the man became sick and was hospitalized. Howard went to visit him, affording him the care he gave to every member of his church. The man became so convicted by Howard's compassion that he apologized for the way he had been treating his pastor.[29]

PUTTING HIS LIFE ON THE LINE

Howard also faced battles of a different kind. One time, an angry husband kidnapped him. He had been counseling a woman who attended the church. Her husband did not attend church and became irate that his wife was telling her troubles to her pastor. The husband met Howard in the church parking lot late one afternoon and asked him to get into the car. Howard complied. The man drove to a remote place outside of the city and said, "Get out of the car!" As he got out, Howard noticed that the man was holding a shotgun! "I'm going to kill you!" he announced. Howard was convinced that his life was over. Just at that moment, another car drove up. It was the man's wife. Howard had no idea she had followed them. She told her husband to put the gun back in the car and go home. Thankfully, he complied! The woman took her shaken pastor back to the church.[30]

A disturbed man came to South one Sunday morning and locked himself in a bathroom. He was carrying a loaded gun and made it known that he intended to take his life. The men of the church called for their pastor. While they hid around the corner, Howard boldly walked to the door. Standing by the door, he began to plead with the man: "We love you! Don't hurt yourself. We'll get you help. You don't need to do this! Please come out and hand me the gun." Approximately twenty minutes later, the man came out. Howard gave him a hug while one of the deacons quickly took the gun. True to his word, Howard provided counseling for the troubled soul.[31]

Howard was a gentle man who avoided trouble. At times, however, he would exhibit tremendous courage in his concern for others. He once put himself in harm's way to rescue an abused woman. After hearing about another incident of violence, Howard went straight to the abuser's house and said to him, "Why don't you hit me instead of hitting your wife?" The man was taken back by such boldness and sought professional counseling.[32] "We are the salt of the earth and shouldn't be surprised to find ourselves in the soup," Howard would say.[33]

James tells us to "Consider it pure joy, my brothers, whenever you face trials of many kinds, because you know that the testing of your faith develops perseverance. Perseverance must finish its work so that you may be mature and complete, not lacking anything" (James 1:2–4). Battles have their place in the life of a servant of God. In fact, they are essential. "A Christian is like a teabag. He isn't worth much until he's been through hot water."[34]

It takes great courage to persevere through difficult times, and no one can maintain a successful ministry in a church for over thirty-five years without some opposition. Howard's faith in God and love for people took him through times of difficulty. But his greatest battle lay ahead when, with his declining effectiveness, the time came for him to retire.

END NOTES

1. Personal interview with Dr. Warren Wiersbe, January 2003.

2. Personal interview with Dr. Ted Ward, August 2002.

3. Personal interview with Dr. Sam Hoyt, February 2002.

4. Personal interview with Harold Gazan, November 2002.

5. Personal interview with Dr. Ted Ward, August 2002.

6. Personal interview with Dr. Sam Hoyt, February 2002.

7. Personal interview with Dr. Ted Ward, August 2002.

8. Personal interview with Dr. Sam Hoyt, February 2002.

9. Personal interview with Harold Gazan, June 2002.

10. Personal interview with Dr. Warren Wiersbe, January 2003.

11. Ibid.

12. Ibid.

13. Personal interview with Harold Gazan, June 2002.

14. Personal interview with Dr. Warren Wiersbe, January 2003.

15. Personal interview with Dr. Sam Hoyt, February 2002.

16. Personal interview with Harold Gazan, November 2002.

17. Personal letter from Dwight Bell, February 2002.

18. Personal letter from Jim Hunsucker, Sr., January 2003.

19. Ibid.

20. Personal interview with Dr. Warren Wiersbe, January 2003.

21. Ibid.

22. Personal letter from Caroll Roost, October 2002.

23. Personal interview with Harold Gazan, June 2002.

24. Personal interview with Rev. Don Dewey, January 2003.

25. Ibid.

26. Personal interview with Dr. Ted Ward, August 2002.

27. Personal letter from Howard Sugden to Dwight Bell, July 29, 1970.

28. Personal interview with Dr. Warren Wiersbe, January 2003.

29. Ibid.

30. Personal interview with Dr. Sam Hoyt, February 2002.

31. Ibid.

32. Ibid.

33. Howard Sugden. *Be Of Good Cheer.* A booklet compiled and published by Bev Shepperson: Lansing, Michigan; 1987.

34. Ibid.

CHAPTER 13

A GRAND WELCOME HOME

Getting old is a bad habit that a busy man has no time for.
—Howard F. Sugden

GOD sovereignly protected Howard throughout the years. From his brush with death as a teenager, due to a ruptured appendix, until the end of his life, God had been watching over His servant.

This divine protection was evident when Howard took a church group to Israel in March of 1978. Hostilities broke out in Jerusalem between the Palestine Liberation Organization and Israelis. Howard's tour group was caught in the middle. The terrorists had even attacked a German tour bus and killed a photographer. The Americans were greatly concerned. The Israeli government imposed a curfew on all coastal cities, but Howard and his group had to catch a flight out of Tel Aviv. To reach the airport in time, they would risk breaking curfew. They decided to make a run for it. "Our bus driver's name was Job," Sugden recalled. "He almost got boils while driving across the city line." On their way to the airport, armed guards stopped their bus. A soldier boarded the bus, carrying a machine gun. He walked the length of the bus, checking every seat, but never saying a word. Thankfully, they were allowed to continue to Tel Aviv without incident and arrived at the airport with four minutes to spare before curfew. The flight departed on time and the tourists arrived home safely. "There is nothing really exciting about dying on foreign soil," Howard told a local reporter.[1] They were glad for the protection of God.

While ministering at the Canadian Muskoka Conference in the early 1980s, Howard and camp director Richard Holliday were walking the grounds. Suddenly, they were overtaken by a storm. Being far from shelter, they sought refuge under a sixty-foot tall fir tree. Moments later a bolt of lightning hit the tree. Howard and Richard thought they were going straight home to heaven and grabbed each other in fear. Miraculously, they escaped without injury. The next day they went back to the site and found the tree split down the middle from top to bottom.[2]

Another time at Muskoka, Howard suffered a slight heart attack. It was late at night and his main concern was not to disturb the sleep of others! Lucile called for help and Richard Holliday's daughter, Kimberly, who was studying to be a doctor, came to his aid. He was given oxygen, received immediate care, and was taken to a hospital. Upon examining Howard, the doctor concluded that the attack was brought on by extreme fatigue and lack of sleep. Howard was given medication and told to get more rest. Howard's response: "Sleep is greatly over-rated . . . so many people die in bed!" Dr. Suk Chang, a physician and member at South Baptist Church, flew up to Ontario to assist in transporting Howard back to Lansing.[3] Thankfully, Howard appeared to suffer no lasting effects from the incident.

Howard and Lucile also experienced an auto accident in 1974. They were traveling home from Frankenmuth, Michigan, about ninety minutes from Lansing. Howard actually thrown from the car and hit his head on the pavement. An accident of this magnitude often proves fatal, but by the grace of God, Howard survived. He did miss one Sunday, but resumed preaching the following week with a large bandage adorning his bald head.[4]

WALKING WITH GOD

Howard enjoyed a familiar walk with God, having been a Christian now for almost sixty years. He had developed an intimate relationship with his Savior, as illustrated in the following story.

On a wintry evening the Sugdens enjoyed a meal with the Bleil family at a restaurant in Chesaning, Michigan. Their return trip took them down some country roads. The Sugdens sat in the back seat of the car next to the Bleil's daughter, Cindy. Howard and Lucile were holding hands, as was their custom. Howard looked tired and weary, as Cindy recalls. In the quietness of the evening, He breathed a simple prayer, "Lord, show me a deer." Just at that moment, they crested the hill and there, standing by the side of the highway, was the most beautiful deer, complete with a full rack of antlers, looking right at the car and posing in the moonlight for Howard. Cindy remembers, "It was absolutely perfect! I have forgotten many of his great sermons, but I'll never forget that moment, when a tired man who bore a heavy pastoral load made a simple request, and the immediate, gorgeous response of God, who was clearly delighted to please His servant."[5]

DECLINE

Howard's health and preaching were in slow but noticeable decline. He had been preaching for almost sixty years, and his waning skills were evident to his closest friends.[6] People noticed that he was recycling sermons. But Howard continued to push forward. He would say, "Getting old is a bad habit that a busy man has no time for."[7]

While at Muskoka in the 1980s, a group of doctors from the Christian Medical Association attended a meeting to hear Howard preach. Afterward, they discussed the message. Some were not impressed. Howard's folksy humor and his theatrical style seemed outdated. His oratorical style, once his greatest asset, now appeared to some as a liability. His message lacked the depth and logic appealing to a group of educated physicians.

The president of the Medical Association, Dr. Haddon Robinson—a preacher not a physician—encouraged the doctors to take a different perspective. He reminded them that Howard was speaking primarily to an older congregation and that his approach in ministry certainly connected with his audience. He also showed them that his tender care and compassionate concern for these older saints ministered to them in ways that the medical community could not. He told a story of how Howard went, in the middle of the night, to a dying woman's bedside. He gave encouragement and comfort to this individual facing life's greatest challenge. Dr. Robinson said Howard was able to minister to that lady and give her answers to life's most puzzling questions in her hour of need. "If you had been there," Haddon said to the doctors, "she would have asked the same questions of you and you would have no answers. Be thankful that he is doing his part so you can do yours."[8]

A banquet, sponsored by the church board, was given for Howard on April 11, 1987, in honor of his eightieth birthday.

Harold Gazan once again took the lead in paying tribute on behalf of the church:

It is difficult to express briefly the thoughts that would represent the various sentiments of all of us here tonight, Pastor. However, I would like to focus my remarks around the single word: Duty. I am sure that when you were a lad growing up on the farm, the word duty meant drudgery. But that is not its only meaning, nor is it the most accurate meaning of the word. The word carries with it a sense of commitment to responsibility. During your fourscore years, you have demonstrated to us what duty really means. It means devotion to the responsibilities that one has been given. In your case, Pastor, it has been devotion to the work of God. You have shown us that through duty, there is dignity in serving. You have shown us that duty brings its own joys and its own rewards by putting service to others above personal interest. Solomon says in Ecclesiastes 12:13, "Fear God and keep His commandments, for this is the whole duty of man." You, Pastor Sugden, have shown us by your life that duty to God is where happiness really is. This has been your hallmark. You have served God so faithfully among us, your church family. You have so steadfastly communicated the truths of God's Word with eloquence, clarity, and devotion.

There have been great men who have ably served in leadership roles beyond their eightieth birthday: Winston Churchill, Konrad Adenauer, and others. A common trait that runs through their lives is a tremendous sense of duty. General Douglas Macarthur summed it up as he said, "Duty, Honor, Country." Your hallmark, Pastor, is "Duty, Church, and the Word of God." As you often remind us, "It is the Word of God that does the Work of God." Thank you for being our friend and pastor.[9]

The year 1989 was significant for South Baptist Church. In the month of May, the church celebrated its centennial anniversary. A "Homecoming Sunday" was planned, along with many activities, including a reception for former staff and church members. Dr. Malcolm Cronk, the pastor who preceded Howard at South, delivered the morning message on May 7th. Dr. Cronk was Pastor Emeritus of Camelback Bible Church in Scottsdale, Arizona. The celebration lasted throughout the summer and into the fall, with special speakers and concerts.

Howard said to a local reporter, "The times have changed, but we are handling truths that are unchanged. The ministry is demanding work. There are few pastors who are eighty-two and carry a full load of ministry. I'm supposed to be dead! We love the work of the ministry. I love it! I love to teach and I love to preach!" Howard was still quite active. The article described Howard as "a former boxer who never smoked or drank, [he] is spry and quick and keeps in shape by hitting his punching bag; he talks articulately about any subject."[10]

HOW DO YOU TELL A LEGEND TO LEAVE?

Dr. Sugden was eighty-two, and there was no plan to transfer the leadership of the church to another pastor. He gave no indication that he was ready or willing to step down. The chairmen of the deacon and trustee boards, Dr. Charles Webb and Dennis Doolen respectively, were in an unenviable position. They were hearing concerns from the congregation about pastor's declining effectiveness, and yet they loved him and wanted to remain loyal. Attendance was slightly eroding. What should they do for the good of the church and the dignity of their pastor?

A suggestion was made to bring in Dr. Wayne Detzler as Executive Pastor. Detzler had served many years with the Greater Europe Mission and was a favorite of Howard's. As Executive Pastor, he could help during the transition period and perhaps take over as Senior Pastor once Howard retired. Howard was not favorable to the plan. In reality, he was not favorable to any plan of replacing him. He could not acknowledge that it was time to step down.[11]

Lucile had made it known that she wanted her husband to retire, but he resisted. She asked Warren Wiersbe to tell him to retire. Warren's response: "If he won't listen to you, how will he listen to me?"[12]

In the fall of 1989, Webb and Doolen initiated a meeting with their pastor. Their purpose was not to ask for his resignation, but to seek his counsel in establishing a transition plan. They sensed that his days were numbered and felt that he might unravel all the good that he had done if he stayed too long or left with no process in place. The two board chairmen made their way to the Sugden home for a meeting they dreaded.

They were warmly welcomed by the Sugdens and seated in the living room. Before they could say anything, Howard spoke: "The time has come for us to step down. We would like to continue to attend South if that is all right."

It was decided that Howard would become, with board approval, Pastor Emeritus. The two men encouraged both Howard and Lucile to continue teaching their respective Bible classes on Sunday morning. Howard was asked to preach once a month in a Sunday service and serve as Minister of Visitation. All of this was agreeable to the Sugdens. The date was set for Howard to officially retire on the last day of December 1989.[13]

RETIREMENT

A beautiful banquet was planned for December 28th. That night, tributes were given by many people in the congregation in celebration of Howard's thirty-five years of ministry in Lansing. The love and gratitude of the congregation was tangible.

With Lucile standing by his side, Howard said, "You've always been an encouragement to me. We have the privilege of being pastors of the greatest church family there could possibly be. And we thank you for it."

A special book was presented to Howard, signed by President George Bush.[14]

The church board knew that they needed to move Howard's large library from the church to his home if an actual transition of leadership was to take place. As a retirement gift, the church built an extension onto the Sugden home to house his extensive library. The Sugdens gave thousands of volumes to pastors and the Grand Rapids Baptist Seminary. Howard kept several thousand volumes to be placed in his new home study.

An article in the *Lansing State Journal* entitled, "Sixty Years of Love" describes the scene of his last Sunday:

The Reverend Howard Sugden will stand at Lansing's

South Baptist Church pulpit as pastor for the last time today, bringing 60 years of ministry to a close. "Preaching today for the last time as pastor won't be easy," Howard said. "A lot of people are very concerned about my leaving, but when you get to be 82, it's time. All these people are my people. People I know; people I love. We care for each other. I've gone down to my office and just stood there and cried because I'm going to be leaving my folk."[15]

The December 1989 edition of the church newsletter, *The South Post*, focused on Howard's retirement. He said:

The years have passed quickly and always there has been in our hearts a confident assurance that we are in the will of God here at South. There could not be found anywhere, we feel, a church family that has been as faithful, kind and helpful as the family here at South. We regret that the hand of time has made us aware of the need to step aside for other servants of God to carry on the ministry that has been so wonderfully blessed of God.

Tributes were published in *The South Post* from individuals in the congregation:

Pastor Howard Sugden has been our teacher, encourager and friend. He has shown a sincere burden for the cares and needs of his people. His ever positive messages and his faithfulness to God's Word have been the richest of blessings for me. —Dennis G. Doolen, board member.

Joy is having a pastor who cares,
  A sweet and kind answer to prayer.
So many believe,
  Because his thoughtfulness exceeds.
He who preaches the Word,
  God sent to this world.
A pastor full of love,
  Was sent from heaven above . . . our Pastor Sugden.
  —Abigail Rynbrandt, teenager

It would be difficult to underestimate the effect that Pastor Sugden has had on my life and ministry. His teaching demonstrated to a skeptical young student that the study of God's Word was more than interesting—it was exciting! Next, he showed me through his ministry and his lifestyle that God's Word was alive and totally relevant for daily life. Finally, he introduced me to great books on the Bible and forever awakened a hunger in me for serious study. My greatest joy will be to pass on the wonder of Bible study, which he stirred up in me, to the next generation, just as he did so faithfully. —Jim Ellis, Sunday School Teacher

It was difficult for Howard to let go. After a few months, he started using his old vacant study again. Although his books were now in his house, he had thoughts of bringing them back to the church. The church board swiftly moved to remodel his old study into a large boardroom and smaller offices.[16]

A Pastoral Search Committee was formed to look for

Howard's replacement. When a candidate was found, the search committee felt that they had the support of Howard and Lucile. Howard offered the use of his library to the young man. A congregational meeting was announced to vote on the candidate. Excitement for a fresh start was everywhere.

The congregational meeting, however, was contentious. Some spoke publicly about the candidate's deficiencies, including Lucile. Although Howard said nothing, most felt he supported her views. The ensuing vote was not strong enough to encourage the young man to accept the pastorate. Many were discouraged. The Search Committee felt betrayed and considered resigning en masse.

Several leaders of the board and one associate pastor met with the Sugdens. Kindly, they requested that Howard and Lucile not take a public, outspoken role in the future. They were allowed to vote, but should not actively participate in any discussion. Now, Howard and Lucile felt betrayed and hurt.[17]

When Rick Hawks was called as the new pastor in December of 1991, the Sugdens were supportive. Pastor Hawks brought a youthful vision to the church, resulting in new enthusiasm. His new approach unsettled others. The church was in a delicate transition. Howard and Lucile often felt caught in the middle.

FINAL DAYS

"I walked into my study the other morning. I was thinking about my study especially, and my books. And alas, I stood there, in the midst of my books, and I said to myself—This is awful! I was standing in a cemetery! Most of the men who wrote those books in my study are dead, ninety-five percent of them. They are gone. And here I am surrounded by the evidence of change and death; the evidence that everything is passing away."[18] Howard was experiencing a world of unwelcomed changes.

"I have a holy fear," he once said, "that as I near the gates of heaven I may have a lot of things knocked out of my hands that I thought were important."[19]

He occupied his time speaking to pastors in various conferences when he was able. Whether it was the early onset of Alzheimer's or simply dementia setting in, Howard began repeating himself as he spoke, using the same illustration more than once in the same sermon.

In the summer of 1992, Warren and Betty Wiersbe came to visit the Sugdens. Warren was speaking at Gull Lake and they wanted to take Howard and Lucile with them. After the service, the men went to a bookstore a short distance from the conference. Just like old times. But it wasn't.

Howard stood in front of a shelf of books, pulled out a volume and said to Warren, "Do you have this book?" "Yes, I do," replied Warren. Howard put the book back. Moments later, he pulled out the very same book and said, "Warren, do you have this book?" Warren answered, "Yes, Howard. I do have that book." Howard put it back on the shelf. Howard repeated the process over and over. How sad it was to see this servant of God decline.[20]

His health began to swiftly deteriorate in 1993. A nurse was coming regularly to the house to care for him. Sylvia and her children were helping Lucile. The family, no longer able to care for his needs, was finally forced to place Howard in a nursing home.

In July 1993, a special service of tribute was held at the Miller Road Bible Church in Lansing. Howard had befriended Pastor Bill Barber over the years. Bill had taken it upon himself to visit Howard every week during the last year. Warren Wiersbe spoke at the service. Howard was in a wheelchair at the time, attended by a nurse. During the service he was sitting in a side room off the platform, where he could see the speaker but could not be seen by the audience. After the service, he was wheeled down to the main floor as people came to greet him and express their love. He feebly smiled and uttered words that few could understand.[21]

Three months later, on the morning of October 14th, Howard was promoted to heaven.

FUNERAL

"What is the death rate in Lansing?" someone once asked Howard. He replied: "It is one apiece. All men's footsteps lead to the grave. Jesus Christ's alone lead out."[22]

Lucile observed, "It's so easy to depend on someone else for your spiritual life. I found that out when my husband passed away. I depended on his prayers so much. I do miss him and his prayers. We did everything together: we worked together, we did our calling together, we studied together, and we read together. We did everything together. But now I am on my own and I will have to lean on God."[23]

The Sunday following Howard's home going, South Baptist held a special service of praise and prayer in his honor. In the obituaries, the newspaper announced:

The Pastor Emeritus of South Baptist Church, Dr. Howard F. Sugden, died Thursday. He was 86. The Reverend Sugden was a legend in this community. Doris Seger, Howard's secretary for 50 years, was quoted as saying: "He had such a love for people and books. He read morning, noon and night. His love for books was only surpassed by his love for people, and his greatest gift was encouraging others."[24]

On a bright Monday morning, October 18th, a crowd gathered for Howard's memorial service. Rick Hawks, the pastor of South Baptist, said, "If there was ever one whose heart was fixed on heaven it was Dr. Sugden."[25] Howard had served South for almost forty years, thirty-five years as its pastor, and four years as Pastor Emeritus.

His good friend from Grand Rapids Baptist Seminary, Dr. Wilbur Welch, called Howard "a great man of God, a personal friend and a much-desired speaker at the school."[26]

Richard Holliday, from the Muskoka Conference, declared: "In my view, [Howard] was the greatest example of how a pastor should show the love of Jesus Christ to needy hearts."[27]

Howard and Lucile's granddaughter, Cindy Blanche, represented the family as she read a poem she wrote entitled "Tears."

Sylvia Sillman, the Sugdens' daughter, wrote: "He Walked with God."

> *He had four loves throughout his life,*
> *The first is God, the second his wife.*
> *A family he cradled to his breast,*
> *Volumes of books read with great zest.*
> *His life on earth was that of a saint,*
> *Of toil and trouble, ne'er a complaint.*
> *The pulpit was where he spread God's word,*
> *Of how salvation could be assured.*
> *When the angels came to take him home,*

Heaven lit up for him alone.
A golden crown he surely must wear,
 He sings with the heavenly choir up there.
I loved him and do miss him so much,
 The kiss on my cheek, his gentle touch.
In my heart I shall ever be glad,
 God gave me the privilege to call him "Dad."

His good friend, former parishioner and co-minister, Rev. Desmond Bell, sang, "He Giveth More Grace." The congregation belted out Howard's favorite hymn, "A Mighty Fortress Is Our God."

The bulletin for the memorial service contained one of Howard's favorite poems:

Not 'til the loom is silent and the shuttles cease to fly,
 Will God unroll the canvas and explain the reason why,
The dark threads are as needful in the pattern He has planned,
 As the threads of gold and silver in our Savior's blessed hand.

In his message, Dr. Warren Wiersbe compared Howard to David, using Acts 13:36 as his text: "After he had served his own generation by the will of God, he fell asleep."

Warren said, "David labored for God as a servant, a shepherd, a soldier, and a singer, and Howard did as well.

"His great motivation was to be a servant. In a day when our churches are embarrassed by celebrities who never learn to be servants, we thank God for the long life and ministry of one whose heart had integrity and whose life manifested sanctity. He was a man of the book. He read the book. He studied the book. He preached the book.

"He loved to sing and could quote hymns by the yard; and he would do it at the strangest times. I remember the time when we were visiting in Great Britain in 1971. We went to the city of Anwoth where the ruins of Samuel Rutherford's church are lying. The great hymn "The Sands of Time Are Sinking" was written from his letters. I can still see Howard, standing in the ruins, as he began to say:

> *Fair Anwoth by the Solway,*
>   *To me thou still art dear!*
> *E'en from the verge of Heaven*
>   *I drop for thee a tear.*
> *Oh! If one soul from Anwoth*
>   *Meet me at God's right hand,*
> *My Heaven will be two Heavens,*
>   *In Immanuel's land.*

"He served his generation well, and there are people all over this world serving God because of the Sugdens' faithful labors.

"And now he sleeps. No one is afraid of sleep. Sleep merely gets you ready for the next day's job."[28]

His job? Perhaps Howard would say, "My new job is much like my old job . . . 'Praising My Savior, All the Day Long!'"

In Lansing, Michigan, on a simple stone in the Deepdale Cemetery, is this modest marker:

Pastor
Howard F. Sugden
"He Walked with God"
1907–1993

END NOTES

1. *Lansing State Journal.* "Crisis to Crisis: Tour strains church group." Lansing, Michigan; March 1978.

2. Personal interview with Dr. Richard Holliday, November 2001.

3. Ibid.

4. Personal letter from Dwight Bell, February 2002.

5. Personal letter from Cindy Bleil Rathnam, February 2002.

6. Personal interview with Harold Gazan, November 2002.

7. Personal letter from Elaine Andrews, September 2002.

8. Personal interview with Dr. Haddon Robinson, January 2002.

9. Harold Gazan. Tribute to Dr. Howard F. Sugden. April 11, 1987.

10. *Lansing State Journal.* Lansing, Michigan; May 6, 1989.

11. Personal interview with Dr. Charles Webb, February 2003.

12. Personal interview with Dr. Warren Wiersbe, February 2002.

13. Personal interview with Dr. Charles Webb, February 2003.

14. Howard Sugden. *Sugden Retirement Banquet-Video.* Held at Michigan State University's Kellogg Center; December 28, 1989.

15. *Lansing State Journal.* Lansing, Michigan; December 31, 1989.

16. Personal conversation with Dennis G. Doolen, May 1996.

17. Personal letter from Harold Gazan, August 1997.

18. Howard Sugden. *God Has the Answers.* A sermon delivered at South Baptist Church, Lansing, Michigan; August 24, 1986.

19. Howard Sugden. *A Call to Advance.* A sermon delivered at South Baptist Church, Lansing, Michigan; January 24, 1988.

20. Personal interview with Dr. Warren Wiersbe, February 2003.

21. Personal letter from Dwight Bell, February 2002.

22. Personal letter from Elaine Andrews, September 2002.

23. Personal interview with Lucile Sugden, September 2001.

24. *Lansing State Journal.* Lansing, Michigan; October 16, 1993.

25. Rick Hawks. *Funeral Service for Howard F. Sugden.* Conducted at South Baptist Church, Lansing, Michigan; October 18, 1993.

26. Dr. Wilbert Welch, Ibid.

27. Dr. Richard Holliday, Ibid.

28. Dr. Warren Wiersbe, Ibid.

SERMONS

THE following three Sugden sermons are taken from different decades and represent some of Howard's favorite pulpit subjects: Bible biography, God's compassion toward sinners, and the wonderful Word of God.

To perserve their original character, these sermons are printed as they were preached.

Jacob—The Man with the Limp

1 Samuel
Delivered at Moody Founders Week
February 1954

YOU saw him yesterday. It may have been in the busy thoroughfare, at the subway station. There were the milling crowds and suddenly he stepped out from all the rest—this man with a limp. The very moment you saw him you began to think all that this meant…Korea, North Africa, Germany. You heard the roar of bombers, the cries of the wounded, the moan of the dying. Then he was lost again in the crowd. But you'll not forget him. Every day you meet these men—men who are marked with a limp.

When the apostle Paul climaxed his letter to the Galatian Christians, a letter defending his own position as an apostle, he contrasted the marks of the Judaizers, that cost nothing, with the marks that he bore in his own body for Jesus Christ—the beatings with rods, the stripes, the imprisonments, the shipwrecks, and he said, "I bear in my body the marks of the Lord Jesus. There is something different about me."

When Robert Murray McCheyne stirred Scotland, someone asked how he preached. "Well," was the reply, "when he preached he wept over the sins of his people and in his study he wept over his own sins and failings." When McCheyne died, kind hands took the books that had been his tender friends off the shelves and gathered together his belongings. They came across letters that only McCheyne had seen. "Dear Mr. McCheyne," read one, "it isn't the way you preached or the message that you brought that led me to Jesus Christ. But it was something about your life that led me to come to Christ." McCheyne was a marked man.

The great desire, I am sure, of each one of us here is not to become great men and great women, to have our names lauded, to be in the limelight of this world. But there is a desire in our hearts that we shall go back to our pulpits, back to our homes, back to our classes, God-marked men.

Jacob had been gone from his old home for twenty years. When he went away, he carried all his belongings in his briefcase. He left because he had cheated, because he had swindled, because he was a hated, hunted man. Now God appeared to him and said, "Get thee back to thine own country and to the land that I have given thee." He gathered Rachel and Leah and the children about him and told them that he was going back to the land of his fathers.

You've heard about mother-in-law trouble, but Jacob had father-in-law trouble. Jacob had swindled Esau, he had practiced deception. It is a strange law in the economy of God that somehow we seem to reap what we sow. Jacob has been deceived and these twenty years have been hard years.

Now in the night he prepares to leave. I can see Rachel. Rachel was her father's daughter and the cunning of Laban was in her. She took a family god off each shelf before they scurried away. Morning comes and Laban misses the gods along with

Jacob. I think he wondered when he saw Jacob was missing, what else was missing. Then he found that the gods were gone. It is an awful thing to have your gods stolen and so he pursues and overtakes them.

He says, "Where are the gods you stole?"

Of course Jacob did not know that Rachel had them. "Why" Jacob says, "you do what you want to with the person you find these gods with."

Rachel is so clever. She sits on those gods, and when Laban her father comes her way she says, "My lord, I am so sorry that my arthritis is bad; I just can't get up this morning."

Then Jacob makes the plea and Laban kisses Jacob and they give that wonderful benediction, "The Lord watch between me and thee, when we are absent one from another." And Jacob says, "You stay on your own side of the fence, you old scoundrel and I'll stay on mine and if l catch you on my side I'll clump your head! Mizpah!"

Laban leaves and as Jacob watches him go in the distance, he shades his eyes and he can almost see Esau coming with four hundred trained men. Laban's hosts leave. Esau's hosts are on the way. Suddenly Jacob sees God's hosts. Oh, how wonderful, that in the hour of his need there were God's hosts. Jacob's company continues on its journey.

The spies that Jacob sent out return and the message that they bring about Esau causes Jacob's heart to fear. It is worse than he expected. Then Jacob begins to pray. Ellicott points out, as does quaint John Trapp, that this is the first recorded prayer in the Bible. Oh, how Jacob reminds God of all the promises and he leaves it in God's hands. God is responsible for his being there. I like prayers like that, don't you?

Some years ago, we were having a prayer meeting for rain down in Indiana. Although we had come to pray for rain, there wasn't a saint that brought an umbrella, not one. We had gone through the first part of the prayer session, which matched the weather conditions—dry—when suddenly back of me a man began to pray. I knew who it was; Mr. Sunday had dropped into the meeting. Well, he did just what Jacob did; he reached out and took all the promises that God had made, I think and he turned them in God's face as if to say, "You said You would do it. Now do something about it. Amen." If I'd had an umbrella, I would have stuck it up right on the spot. I just knew that we would have rain and we did.

Jacob prayed, and when he had finished praying he did exactly what most of us do—he started planning. He said, "Now, I'm sure that God could do this, but if God doesn't, I had better see if I can't help myself out of the mess I'm in." Oh, the wonder of it. He is going to appease Esau. He is going to make him a present, and he is going to cover Esau's face—for that is the same word. It is the word from which we get the word "atonement."

In this we see . . .

JACOB'S CONCERN

His chief concern, of course, was to save Jacob, save self, keep his position. He calls his men, and takes 220 goats, 220 sheep, 60 camels, 50 cattle, and 30 asses, and he puts them in five separate droves. He knows that when Esau meets these droves, with characteristic oriental brevity he will say, "Whose servants art thou? Where art thou going? Whom do these belong to?" Jacob instructs his servants to say, "They be thy ser-

192

vant Jacob's. They are a present for thee, and Jacob is coming." Say, five droves! A lot of value wrapped up in this. Jacob's a rich man. God has blessed him.

I find, and I am sure you do, so much of Jacob in God's people. The concern that Jacob had is so often the concern of God's people. Self—self is the great enemy. Not Esau, not the board of deacons, not the board of trustees, not the orneriness of people—but self.

I love the book of Job, and I am sure you have found, as I have, that the heart of Job's trouble was not boils—but Job. This was the problem of the great apostle in Romans 7. Someone asked Spurgeon if he was not troubled about the Pope. Spurgeon said, "The pope I have the most trouble with is Pope Spurgeon."

This is Jacob's concern as he begins his plans—self-preservation, self-esteem, self-expression, self-praise. Self is like the Dead Sea, everything flowing in. This was Jacob up to this moment. When he was born, you will remember, he was grabbing. The next thing we see him doing is getting. Everything coming Jacob's way. That was his concern.

Now the nightshades are about to fall. Jacob has sent the presents on ahead to protect himself, and he takes Leah and Rachel and the servants and the children, and they cross the brook Jabbok. Where they crossed, I understand, the ravine is wide, perhaps three or four miles, before the high banks along the edge of the river are mounted. He takes Rachel and Leah and the others up the bank. He builds a fire for them and then he goes back beside the brook along the river plains of Jabbok. It's wilderness country—trees, wooded places. Jacob is alone.

How much has been wrought out when men have been

alone. Moses was alone and the voice of God called from the burning bush, "Moses!" Job was alone when he caught a glimpse of the Lord and he cried, "I have heard of thee by the hearing of mine ear: but now mine eye seeth thee." Isaiah was alone, and he saw the Lord high and lifted up. Habakkuk was alone and he heard the Lord say, "The just shall live by faith." Nicodemus was alone and he heard, "Ye must be born again." The woman at the well was alone and she heard Jesus say, "I that speak unto thee am He."

It's so hard to get alone these days, isn't it? You think you're going to get alone, and then Willie's nose needs wiping; Mary is in trouble; there's the phone ringing; there's the serial story on the radio. The days slip away and we are not alone with God, the world forgotten.

JACOB'S CONFLICT

But Jacob is alone, and in that night suddenly there is a snap of a twig. Jacob thinks that Esau is there, because up to this time Esau is his enemy, and his concern is about Esau. Out of the shadows comes a Man, and the Man wrestles with Jacob. That's the way the Word says it. It does not say Jacob wrestled, but the Man wrestled. There was something this Man was trying to get for Jacob.

On through the night they wrestle. Jacob is a fair antagonist. He did not know all the holds, but he had not led a shepherd's life for nothing, and self is strong in Jacob.

Then suddenly this unknown assailant reaches down and touches Jacob's thigh and self is broken. Jacob had tricked dear old Isaac, and he put it over on Esau, but he could not do it with God. He has found One who is more clever than he.

God knows all the holds. Jacob's conflict comes to an end. He is broken.

Did you ever think that before God makes men, God breaks men? There is Saul—a broken will on the road to Damascus; broken desires in Philippians 3, "Things that were gain to me . . ."; broken health in 2 Corinthians 12—Paul is broken but blessed.

Jacob's concern, Jacob's conflict—not with Esau but with God, and now . . .

JACOB'S CONFESSION

The Man said to Jacob, "Who art thou?" As though He did not know. He had seen Jacob when he grabbed Esau's heel. He had seen all of those things that had happened during those twenty years. "Who are thou?" Well, if this had been the previous chapter, the answer would have been, "I am a good shepherd; I have taken care of the flocks; I . . . I. . . ." But now Jacob cries out of his crushed self, "I am Jacob!" That's who I am— crook, deceiver, supplanter. Say anything you want to say about me, I am Jacob!

I have discovered that you can get men to say, "I am a fundamentalist." "I am an Anglican." "I am a Methodist." "I am a Baptist." "I am a Presbyterian." But how few there are who will say, "I am Jacob!" Oh, to have at the beginning of life the right conception of self, that self is nothing.

There are four "ends" mentioned in the Scripture. There is the end of the law in Romans 10:4; there is the end of sins in Daniel 9:24; there is the end of the Lord in James 5:11 [i.e., the final outworking of God's plan]; but in Genesis 6:13 the Lord speaks about the end of all flesh. The Lord says that the end of all flesh is judgment, condemnation. Oh, to know that in our flesh there dwells no good thing; to have no confidence in the flesh; to recognize that we are only evil continually. Man in the flesh cannot please God. I am Jacob.

Can you say it this morning? Your concern has been about yourself. You have had some conflicts. You have been criticizing God. God has been wrestling. What a confession—I am Jacob. No wonder Elihu said, "If any man will say, 'I have sinned,' God will say, 'Quick—deliver him!'"

JACOB'S CONQUEST

"Thy name shall be called no more Jacob, but Israel."

A new name—no longer the old supplanter, no longer the old deceiver, but a man who is a prince with God. Thou art— oh, put your name in there this morning. Thou art Jim; thou shalt be—Thou art Mary; thou shalt be—Thou art—Thou shalt be—A new name.

But then Jacob cries, "Who are you? What is your name?" A new desire was wrapped up in this simple statement, to know the name of this Man. It was the desire of the great apostle— "That I may know him."

The sun begins to mount over the eastern horizon and there is a new day. The night is past, the mists have cleared, the smell of the freshness of a new morning has come and there is a new name, a new desire and a new day. It sounds like Exodus, doesn't it? "This shall be the beginning of months for you."

But there is also a new walk. Jacob limped. Can't you see it now? There is the little group gathered around the campfire in the cool of the morning and suddenly one of the boys shades his eyes and says, "There comes Dad!" And Leah says, "He is limping! Something must have happened to him last night."

"I met God," says Jacob. "I no longer am Jacob, but a prince with God. There is a new name, a new desire, a new day and I'll never walk the same again."

You remember that next day when they went out to meet Esau, Jacob—Israel, I should say—arranged those bands. He put the servants first and next he put Leah and her children and then he put Rachel and little Joseph. And Jacob—Jacob is not behind, but he walks in front of the group, and he goes to meet Esau. I think the thing that startled Esau was Jacob's limp. He was a God-marked man.

God-marked men may we be.

Amen.

GOD NEVER GIVES UP

Luke 15
Delivered at South Baptist
June 5, 1966

IF you were handed a pencil and asked to describe in 100 words or less the activity of God, what would you say God is doing? If you were an artist and had your easel and could dip your brush in all the glorious colors, how would you paint the portrait of God? Men are doing this today, sad to say. It is being done in all our popular magazines, in our periodicals; everybody is dipping his brush and dipping his pen and saying nasty things about God. But most of these folk know very little about God. For I would remind you that if you know one single truth about God, you know it because it is in His Word, the Holy Bible. All that God has revealed about Himself He has revealed in His Word. And the revelation is confined completely to His Word. You do not know God because you've had a "funny feeling" or a vision at midnight. The only truth you know about God is the truth He has revealed in His Word. And I declare to you on the authority of the Word of God, that God's one activity in this present hour in which we live is the activity of searching out men and finding men and bringing men to Himself. This is the activity of God. And this has been the activity of God throughout history.

And the activity of God in history has been wrought out by the church and by believers who make up the church.

When we look into God's Word and find the first portrait of God acting in relation to men, what is God doing? He's looking for them. You only have to pass through the first two chapters and arrive at Genesis 3 to find God searching, looking for a man who has run away and hidden from Him.

Now in Genesis 5, we find ourselves in the middle of a graveyard. On every stone there is a simple epitaph, just two words: "He died." I was in a local cemetery just yesterday. From every grave came one message: "he died," "she died." But look! Right in the middle of Genesis 5, what does God do? He reaches down and He finds a man, and that man's name is Enoch. And the Bible says that "Enoch walked with God." There was something different about Enoch after God found him.

In Genesis 13 there begins a record that continues for some forty chapters of a man named Abraham and his descendents. Do you know what Isaiah later said about Abraham? He said, "God found Abraham." That's all He did, He just found him. When you read the life of David, this is how the psalmist sums up the story of David, "I have found a man." As the ministry of God unfolds in His Word, He is finding men.

Now I believe that the account in the Old Testament of God finding men carries over into the New Testament, and it is nowhere more wonderfully told than in Luke 15. Someone has said that this, without doubt, is the greatest portion of the Word of God and the greatest story every told. It all happened on a day when the Lord Jesus was teaching. And he was teaching as no other man could teach. He was teaching about people counting the cost. He said, chapter 14, "Did you ever start in to build a building and never have figured out how much it was going to cost?" And he talked of buildings and of family and of life and warfare, and he said, "I call men now to come to me and to sacrifice and to do battle and to give." I have always thought this kind of preaching would drive people away. But when the Lord Jesus turned to the crowd and said if a man comes after me and does not hate his father and mother, let him go away. If he comes to me and isn't involved in a battle with the elements that are against him, let him go. And you know what happened? The crowds came. You see, Christianity is lost today because it's lost its challenge. It has become anemic, weak. The average church is just getting by. The Lord said, "It's a conflict, it's a battle, it's a struggle!" And they came. Everybody came—scribes and Pharisees were there. And then it says publicans and sinners came. And those publicans and sinners moved through the crowd. The publicans were a hated bunch and the sinners, they were a bad lot. The scribes and Pharisees were the religious people who knew all the answers. They had added to the Law until it became a burden to them that they couldn't bear. And they stood around and they criticized everybody else. And suddenly, as they saw the sinners and the publicans pushing in to see Jesus, the scribes and Pharisees complained aloud, "We resent this!" And then they said the greatest word that has ever been said about the Lord Jesus. They said, "This man receiveth sinners and eats with them!" They didn't know it, but their criticism was the greatest glory that was ever said about Jesus: "This man receiveth sinners to himself." According to the Greek, Jesus was doing more than saying, "Well, glad to see you, sir! Glad you came in tonight. We're awfully glad to see you tonight." It was more than this. They said, "Do you know what this man is doing? He's taking sinners to Himself!" And when they said this, the Lord Jesus said, "This is so." And if there is any portion of the Word of God that needs to be shouted, and declared, and affirmed, and spread, it is this wonderful fifteenth chapter of the Gospel according to Luke, more glorious in its message than any other portion of the Word of God: "God receives men."

THE PLIGHT OF MAN

Then He spoke a parable to them. The three parables in Luke 15 are really one parable. It is a story of a sheep and a coin and a boy, three ordinary things. And when you read it, you discover they all have one thing in common—they were lost! They were all lost! The coin was lost, and the boy was lost and the sheep was lost. Do you know that this is the common lot of man? And aren't you amazed how God describes it? A sheep and a coin and a boy—they're all lost and they're all different.

Do you know anything about sheep? No sheep ever sat down with his fellow sheep and said, "Fellas, we're gonna take a trip today . . . we're gonna get lost." Sheep never do this! You know what this sheep did? This sheep just started out and went nibbling along in green pastures, and he just got farther and farther away, until he was lost. And what led the sheep astray? His appetites. Appetites lead men and women astray: appetites for sex, for lust, for pleasure, for sin—appetites! No man, when he took the first cocktail, ever thought he was going to be a drunk. No woman, the first night she sold herself, ever thought she'd be a harlot. It's an appetite that leads them astray.

What happened to the coin? Circumstance! You see, any coin falls because gravity pulls it down. And there are some people who never rise above circumstances. They will never be strong enough to overcome. And coins are lost because of the downward pull of things.

We know why the son was lost. He was lost because he was a rebel. And these three pictures describe the condition of the human heart: Lost through fleshly appetites, through the downward pull of flesh and circumstances, and lost through rebellion against God. Everybody was born into the world that way. That's what it means to be lost, lost like the wandering sheep, lost like the fallen coin, lost like the rebellious boy.

But let me suggest to you that theologically there's much more to being lost than you might assume. Because Biblically to be "lost" is to be under judgment. If you are not saved and you do not know Christ as your Savior, you are not waiting to be judged, you are already judged by God. The Word of God says, "He that believeth not, is already condemned" (John 3:18). That puts a different light on it. Somebody said, "Oh, I'll take my chances, I'll wait 'til judgment." You don't need to wait for judgment, you are already judged. To be lost is to be involved in death. By one man sin entered the world, and death by sin, Romans 5:12, "so that death passed upon all men, for all have sinned." A man who is lost is under condemnation and he is involved in death: physical death first, spiritual death, and eternal death—three kinds of death in the Word of God. He is also under the power of the enemy. This is what it means to be lost.

Somebody said to me not long ago, "Well, what does it mean to be lost? You mean you can't find your way back?" Don't be silly! Man is lost like a sheep—his appetites, he's lost like a coin—circumstances, he's lost like a boy—rebellion! And he is under judgment. He is involved in death and he's held in the grip of the enemy. That's what it means to be lost. And it is awful to be lost! The sheep, the coin, the boy all had this in common. And they had something else in common. They were all found.

THE PERSISTENCE OF GOD

Suddenly, right in the midst of this plight of being lost, you have a new idea injected. Notice it in verse 4, the last part of the verse: "He goes after that which is lost until he finds it." Verse 8, the last part: "She seeks diligently until she finds it." Verse 24: "This, my son is found." So in the plight that's presented, you suddenly are aware of the persistence of God.

Now God is likened first of all to a shepherd. And this is a picture of the Son. He's a shepherd, and this shepherd goes after the sheep that was lost until he finds it. He goes after it. The woman is the Spirit of God. In the Word of God, the church is likened to a bride, and here's the woman sweeping. And she sweeps until she finds it. The father watches for his son until he returns. So suddenly you are aware that lost man in this social revolution that he finds himself in today, in Vietnam, in Africa, in the United States, out in New York City, in San Francisco, in Chicago with its gaiety and its lights, that man is being pursued by God. And the whole Godhead is involved in it. The Son seeks as the shepherd, the Spirit sweeps like the woman, and the Father waits. And did you know that if you have come to His Word and you are not a Christian, that you cannot turn and go your way without being aware of this: that God is mightily interested in your life? And God's is no passive interest. The shepherd looking and looking, the woman sweeping, the father waiting and watching.

Now if you stopped here, you'd only get half of it. Because the fact is that man is in a plight. He is lost and God has taken cognizance of his lost condition and God has moved to find him. And the whole Trinity is involved in the work of salvation. It is more than raising a hand—oh, that may be part of it. But it is the deep searching work of the Spirit of God that brings our hearts to a place where they are open to receive Christ. But there's more than this.

WHAT IS THE POINT OF ALL THIS?

I've lived in this chapter for many years. What really is the point of it? You have the plight and the persistence. What's the point of it? What is God saying in this?

First of all, He's saying, concerning the sheep, that the shepherd went out to seek for the sheep and he sought until he found him. Do you know why? Because he loved him! That's all. You can never understand this until you can understand an oriental shepherd. And the whole thrust of this is simply that God loves you! No wonder when Mr. Moody heard Henry Morehouse preach for five straight nights on the "Love of God" he was startled. You see, God loves us. God loves you, and He uses the illustration of the shepherd to tell you that He loves you. And He uses a coin because he wants you to see that you are of infinite value to Him. Mark it down so that it will never be forgotten in your mind, that this parable of God the Father, and God the Spirit, and God the Son working in the lives of men is not only to display the love of God, but to show that you are of value to God! What a dignity this puts in life. I am of value to God. There are some things that God cannot do in this world without YOU! And regardless of who you may be, He takes your personality into His hands and He says, "You're of value to me!" And I do not care what your position in life may be. Maybe you wash dishes for a living. I washed dishes in the college cafeteria. What a hot and awful job. But I came to realize that I was of value to God, right there in that kitchen washing dishes. Maybe you drive a truck. Whatever you do, you are of value to God. And when you realize this, you can do whatever you do to the glory of God.

So He uses a sheep to show His love for us, and He uses a coin to show our great value. Why do you think He uses the illustration of the boy? He uses the boy to show that even the worst can be saved—because this boy was the worst. Do you know the worst thing that could ever happen to a Jewish man? That's right, slopping pigs. He could not have gone much lower than that. He had taken what his father gave him, gone into a far country, given himself over to evil, wasted everything he had, and now he's slopping pigs, and he's so hungry he's tempted to eat the garbage he's feeding the pigs.

I think of my friend J. C. Massey, a huge man, tall, with long white hair that hung down around his shoulders. He was a pastor of Tremont Temple. He said to me one day, "Howard, I've won more souls with my right hand than most people have ever imagined. I've loved people into the kingdom of God." I'll never forget that. He said, "Don't be too high and mighty to get down and put your arm around your people and tell them you love them." Old Massey would take his sound truck and park the truck on the edge of the red light district. He said to me, "Many nights, Howard, I stood out on that sound truck and I shouted over my loudspeaker system to the harlots in the red light district, 'Ladies, God loves you!' " And he said, "I've seen the windows go up in the apartments. And I've had women march out of their apartments and down to my sound truck because God saves even the worst sinners!" He must save even the worst; He saved me. The plight—lost! The persistence—until! The point—God's love and value for even the worst!

THE PRAISE OF HEAVEN

The sheep and the coin and the boy; they were all found. And do you know what happened when each was found? There was praise and rejoicing. I found out that a shepherd, an oriental shepherd, in the days of the Lord Jesus, was a shepherd who took care of a community's flocks. Sometimes a little town of 600 or 700 people would have one shepherd to take care of all their flocks. And they tell me that this weather-beaten face, this man with the tear in his eye, this man who looked like a prophet, was one of the loved men of his little town. He cared for the sheep. And when it was noised about in the evening time that one of the sheep was lost, the whole little community turned out to wait for the shepherd to come back. And they knew he wouldn't come back until he had the sheep. He loved the sheep! And when that little community peered through the gathering gloom of an oriental evening and saw this weather-beaten prophet with his long robe pulled back and a lamb in his arms, they began to sing and to give thanks and to praise. And do you know what the Word of God says? It says that's what happened in the presence of the angels when I was saved. A yellow-haired teenage boy in a little Baptist church, and heaven is all astir because the lost has been found!

So it is about the joy over one sheep that's returned. It is about the joy that a woman finds in her heart when she has

206

found her most treasured possession. The coin, you see, was what kept her from being just a woman spoken of in ill favor in the streets. This coin was like her engagement ring. And then she had lost it. She had lost her warrant of purity, and when she found it, there was praise in her heart. And when the son came back, there was praise in the father's heart because the son had returned!

A FINAL PLEA

But here is something very interesting. It doesn't say one single thing about the sheep doing anything. The shepherd went out to seek for the sheep. It doesn't say there was a little sheep out there looking for the shepherd. It just says that he was lost and the shepherd went after him. The coin didn't get up on its side and stand on its thin edge and say "Yoo-hoo! Here I am!" It was just lost!

But when it comes to a living personality, suddenly you discover that God begins to bring circumstances into that life. Now we are rescued like a sheep, we are found like a coin, but we're more than sheep and coins. We are living personalities. So God has to begin a work in our lives to deal with us and bring us to the place of our decision for him. So what does he do?

In the case of the boy, the first thing he did was to take away his bankbook. He awakened one morning and everything was gone. Every earthly thing he trusted in was smashed to a thousand pieces. And then he began to think about God. And if he hadn't begun to think about God, where would he be yet? He would be out in the pig pen. I don't know where I would be if God hadn't allowed some circumstances to come into my life.

Maybe you are not yet saved and God has been dealing with

you for years? Don't you wonder sometimes what more God will have to do to make you decide for him? He just took this man who had gone away from home. He had all that his father had. He'd lived upon that and he'd spent it all freely, and then suddenly he found himself stripped of everything. And when God stripped him, God began to work. You say, "Did God have anything to do with the circumstances?" God allowed the circumstances. And when God allowed the circumstances, he came to himself and said, "I'd like to go back to Father's house."

If you have never personally received Christ, you're lost. You're lost. You may be nice and lovely and gracious, but you're lost. You're as lost as the sheep, you're as lost as the coin, and you're as lost as the boy. Maybe some circumstance has come into your life, and God is talking to you personally.

Over 30 years ago, Mrs. Sugden and I began to preach in a little town not far from this city. The undertaker lived right across the street from us. One day, the undertaker said to me, "Did you hear what happened this morning?" I said, "No, tell me." "Oh," he said, "We had a tragedy this morning." I said, "What was the tragedy?" He said, "In the little town up the highway, a father backed out of his garage this morning and didn't know that his little boy had wandered out into the driveway, and he killed him." He said, "The little boy is over at the undertaking parlor." Two weeks passed by and one evening there was a rap on our door. I went to the door and there was a young couple. They said, "Could we come in and talk with you?" We said, "Yes." I said, "Tell me your names." When they told me their names, it clicked. This was the family that had lost the little boy. They came in and sat down. They said, "You know our little boy was killed?" "Yes." And they said, "In this circumstance God has dealt with us." They had become saved. Of course I don't believe that God killed the little boy to save his parents. But it happened, and God was able to use it to point them to their need of Christ. And this is what he did with the prodigal son. Things went against him, and in the hour of his being stripped of everything, he found out that God could meet his need.

Has God been dealing with you, dear friend? Has He? If He has, and you are not saved, God looks for you today as He looked for a sheep, as He looked for a coin, and as He looked for a boy. And I pray that He may find you, and that you may come to Him.

Amen.

God's Greatest Work

Delivered at South Baptist
January 5, 1975

THERE is a lovely, lilting little hymn, which we sometimes still sing, that speaks about God's work:

> *This is my Father's world,*
> *And to my listening ears,*
>   *All nature sings and round me rings*
>   *The music of the spheres.*
>   *This is my Father's world,*
> *Oh let me ne'er forget,*
>   *That though the wrong seems oft so strong,*
>   *God is the Ruler yet.*

When we look out upon creation, it is not difficult to believe that God is at work. He is working in His world. And His work is not confined to nature. The Psalmist said, "His throne reigneth over all."

I believe that. So it's "summer and winter and springtime and harvest"—God at work! He is at work among the nations. David said, in Psalm 75:7, "But God is the judge: He putteth down one and setteth up another." Man, I like that! In His sovereignty, He gives us presidents and queens and kings and governors—God at work!

He is also at work in His church. Never has there been a day when the church has been assailed by its "friends" and enemies as it is today. Volumes—nasty volumes—are being written about the church, in particular about its "social consciousness." May I suggest to you that when all the authors have been laid end to end, the Church of Jesus Christ will go on—for the gates of hell will not prevail against it.

The greatest work that God is doing is not the work that He is doing in nations—great as that is—and in His creation—great as that is. For you and for me personally, the greatest work that God is doing is the work that He is doing in your life and in my life. And that's very personal!

Now when the Lord Jesus prayed His great prayer in John 17:4, he said, "I have finished the work Thou gavest me to do." That work was the work of making possible your redemption and my redemption.

When Peter met with the early church council in Acts 15, he said, "God is taking out of the world a people." That's His work in this day, He is taking out of the world a people. He is not repairing the world, He is not "fixing it up." God is taking out of the world, a people for His name.

Paul says in Philippians 1, that God, who has begun this work of redemption in our lives, will continue it until the day of Jesus Christ. And I believe that! That's the only hope I have—that God doesn't start us and then drop us. God doesn't start us and say, "You didn't last through the day! You're all done!" I don't believe that! God begins a work in us and then He continues it until the day of Jesus Christ.

GOD IS WORKING THROUGH HIS WORD

Now the work that God is doing in relation to man today, He is doing through His Word. And that is what makes this hour of tremendous significance. The work that God is doing He is not doing through imaginary visions or writing in the sky. God is doing His work through His Word. That is the only way that God has of doing it. He could do it through angels. He could do it through IBM, but He doesn't. He is doing it through His Word. I stand in awe at times when I read in God's Word what He says about Himself and about His greatest witness, His Word. In Psalm 12:6 He says, "The words of the Lord are pure words: as silver tried in a furnace of earth, purified seven times." We read in Psalm 19:7, "The law of the Lord is perfect. . . ." Who would dare to say that? The Word of the Lord is a pure Word, the Word of the Lord is a perfect Word. Psalm 119 declares, "Thy Word is very pure: therefore thy servant loveth it." And moving ahead to Proverbs 30, we read in verse 5, "Every word of God is pure. . . ." So here is a Word that declares of itself that it is pure and perfect.

As we read further we note that added to the purity and the perfection of God's Word is another great quality: stability. Ages change, men change, governments change, churches change, times change, things change. Is God caught up in this? Do we need a new Bible in the middle of the twentieth century? The Psalmist didn't think so. The Lord Jesus didn't think so. Looking again at Psalm 119, we read in verse 89, "Forever O Lord, Thy Word is settled in heaven." And in the same Psalm, verse 144, "The righteousness of Thy testimonies is everlasting. . . ." And in verse 152, "Concerning Thy testimonies, I have known of old that Thou hast founded them forever." As we head toward the

New Testament, we stop at Isaiah 40:8, where we read, "The grass withereth, the flower fadeth: but the Word of our God shall stand forever." Arriving in Matthew's gospel, we hear the words of the Lord Jesus, who stepped out of heaven and came to earth and knew all about God because He is God, knew about the Word of God, and knew about you and me. We hear our Lord declare in Matthew 24:35, "Heaven and earth shall pass away but My words shall not pass away." So here is the Word of God affirming of itself that it is a pure Word and a stable Word, a Word that knows no change. If time goes on for 100 years or 200 years or 300 or 400 years, the unchanging God has given to us an unchanging Word; and it will always be up to date and ahead of us. Always.

THE WORD IS GOD-BREATHED

Now immediately someone asks, "Well how did we get this Word? What process did God pass through to get the Word to us?" May I explain so that you will not misunderstand? We believe that first of all, as we read in 2 Peter, chapter 1, God chose "holy men." When He had chosen these holy men, Isaiah, Jeremiah, Dr. Luke, Peter, and all the others, what did God do? Peter said that when they sat down to write, "they were moved by the Holy Ghost" (2 Peter 1:21) so that they did not write from themselves but from God.

When somebody comes along to you and says, "Oh yes, I know you think that God dropped the Bible on a golden cord." You say that you never heard that in your life! It was never taught in our house of God. We teach that the Word of God was given to us first of all by holy men as God "breathed upon them." Let us see what God said to young Timothy. This is important to understand. What you know and remember about the Word of God will determine the way you treat the Word of God and the way you use the Word of God. In 2 Timothy 3:16 we read, "All Scripture is given by inspiration of God. . . ." Now the root word "inspire" that is used here is an intriguing word. It means to "breathe into," or to "breathe upon." Imagine, God, by the moving of the Holy Spirit, breathed out His Word and breathed it into these men. So the Word of God that I hold in my hand is a "breathed-out" Word—breathed out by God Himself. Believers, you are going to be teaching people and speaking to people, helping them along the road of life in every area. You will have to have an authoritative Word. God has given you an authoritative Word, His own breathed-out Word.

There was a man, unfortunately now dead, by the name of Edward J. Young. A linguist and a scholar, Edward J. Young, in my judgment, was one of the greatest men of this generation. When he died at sixty-two years of age, he had given to us at least five great volumes on Isaiah. His wonderful work *Thy Word is Truth* is the greatest thing that has been written on the subject of the Word of God. Writing on 2 Timothy 3, Dr. Young asks, "What does Paul mean? What can such a strange designation as 'inspiration' or 'breathing out' mean? Why did Paul thus speak of the Scriptures? He thus spoke, we believe, because he wished to make as clear as possible the fact that the Scriptures did not find their origin in man but in God. It was God the Holy Spirit who breathed them forth. They owe their origin to Him. They were a product of the breath of God Himself. It is a strong figure. . . . A strong figure however is needed in order that Timothy may realize that he is being asked to place his confidence not in writings which merely bless the hopes and aspirations of the best of men, but rather in writings, which are actually breathed out by God, and consequently, of absolute authority. We believe this, that the Word of God is an absolute authority. The Scriptures therefore are writings which found their origin in God. They are the very product of His creative breath." It is this then we remember when we speak of the inspiration of the Bible. Now he adds, "We are convinced that the Scriptures do indeed claim to be the Word of God. And since they are from Him and find their origin in Him only, they are therefore infallible and entirely free from error of any kind. Since their author is truth and cannot lie, so His Word, the Scriptures, is truth and cannot lie."

My friends, on His Word I stand. And this is not a popular stance today because this is a day when all authority is being questioned. We look at the president and immediately start searching to see if he dropped a football in the fourth quarter when the game was against them. [Probably an allusion to Gerald Ford, who was president in 1975, and who had played football in college.] A doctor has to go and protect himself against the men who would destroy him. Everybody is under fire today, and I remind you that the Word of God has been and is under fire, and when the fires have cleared away and all the smoke is gone, the Word of our God will stand forever. Oh, I tell you, how thrilling it is to think of the Word of God, how it came to us, a God-breathed book, God's Holy Bible, light divine, its pages gilded by a glory majestic as the sun.

THE WORD OF GOD SAVES US

Now the question is what does the Word of God do? Why is it so important? Does God just give us a book so He can say,

"Well I gave them the book; they've got a book?" Is that why God gave it to us, or does God have a purpose in the giving of His Word? Let us address this question. Go to 1 Peter 1:22 and mark what is written. "Seeing ye have purified your souls in obeying the truth through the Spirit unto unfeigned love of the brethren, see that ye love one another with a pure heart fervently." Peter is writing to believers and is saying "love one another." And he says, "I'll tell you how it happens that you can love one another. You can love one another because something happened to you." What's happened to believers? We've been born again, born again "not of corruptible seed, but of incorruptible by the Word of God, which liveth and abideth forever," says 1 Peter 1:23. God pictures His Word in amazing ways. Jeremiah says, "Thy Word is like a hammer." I have seen it hammering away at hearts. And he says, "Thy Word is like a fire." It warms our hearts. And now Peter says the Word of God is a seed. A seed is different. The Word of God identifies a seed as that which communicates and has life in itself. The Word of God, the Bible, is a life-communicating book. Men are born again by receiving the Word of God. You are saved because you received the Word of God. That's how you are born again. You are not saved through fuzzy feelings, emotional experiences. Show me where the Bible says that. Men and women are born again by receiving the Word of God. The written Word of God tells of Jesus Christ, the living Word of God. And the only way that man knows about the Lord Jesus Christ is through the written Word. You don't find it in "Popular Mechanics," "Cosmopolitan," or "Better Homes and Gardens." You find it in the Word of God. That is where the Word is found by which we are born again.

So the Bible is a life-communicating Word. That is why at South Church, beginning in our little nurseries and going all the way through our Bible School, we teach the Word of God. There may be men and women in this house of God who have never personally trusted Jesus Christ, who are lost, without hope and without God in the world, people for whom the only means of rescue is hearing the Word of God and believing it. Paul writes, in Romans 10:17, "Faith cometh by hearing and hearing by the Word of God." I am here physically because I was born of a physical seed. But I am here as a Christian because I was born of a spiritual seed: the Word of God. And so we give out the Word. We teach it and hand it out through tracts and writings and letters, and we speak to men on the streets about the Word of God. There is no other way to do God's work except through God's Word.

I have a little letter that I have saved. It's a very short letter, ten words. And it means a lot to me. On a Sunday afternoon five or ten years ago, Sparrow Hospital called. The gracious nurse said, "Pastor Sugden, come quickly, we have got a man who is in deep trouble." I went and found a man, and that man has haunted me ever since. He was caught in two great grips: the grip of a physical habit that had almost slain him and, as a consequence of that habit, he had lost his voice and couldn't talk. He was waiting to get a little device that he could slip in his throat so that later on he could whisper and be heard. I sat by that man, who was without hope and without God. He might have been a millionaire, but a man without hope. He might have been a businessman. But here he was in a desperate hour. And I just read to him the Word of God; and I shall never forget how that man listened. He couldn't talk, so he had a pencil and pad and he wrote notes to me. I talked and he wrote. And what do you think happened? He was saved. The next time I went to see him, he had a little ten-word note written to me, and it said, "I have never felt so good inside in my life." The same thing happened to me when as a teenager I received the Word of God. If you are a believer, the same thing happened to you when you received the Word of God. The same thing will happen if you have come to this house of God and don't know Jesus Christ as Savior. If you believe, it will happen to you, and you will be born again, "not of corruptible seed but of incorruptible by the Word of God that liveth and abideth forever."

THE WORD OF GOD FEEDS US

We are born again by the Word of God. But that is not all. You do not have babies and not do anything with them. My old Scotsman friend said to me, "Howard, it is as important to feed the babies as it is to have them." And he's right, you know. Now how is a spiritual baby that is born again and brought into the family of God going to be fed? The Bible tells us that the food for the spiritual man is the spiritual food of the Word of God. When a man or a woman is saved and then never hears the Word of God, his or her spiritual life becomes anemic and weak and ordinary and flat. A new Christian in that situation begins to wonder, "What is the matter with me; what am I to do?" Turn again to 1 Peter and look at chapter 2, verse 1. The Word of God gives us life; now let's see what else it does. Peter writes, "Wherefore laying aside all malice, and all guile, and hypocrisies, and envies, and all evil speakings, as newborn babes, desire the sincere milk of the Word, that ye may grow thereby." So the same Word that gives us life now becomes the way that God nourishes us and builds us up in our Christian faith. We are born by the Word and we are fed by the Word.

It is amazing how our appetites change. When I was a lad, I used to go to church with my dad and mom. I never missed a Lord's Day in church, and I was always grateful to God that they took me. I wasn't saved until I was nineteen years of age. No one ever talked to me about salvation. I sat in a Sunday school class through my years as a teenager, but not one soul ever said a word to me about Christ. My teacher never said a word to me about Christ. I am sure he looked down and said, "'That Sugden kid is here again, we've got trouble today," and never thought of talking to me about Jesus. Then I got saved. I came to know Christ. And the strangest thing happened on Sunday morning. The church service that had been boring suddenly wasn't boring anymore. And I wondered why they didn't have more church services? I thought, "We have four other days, we could have a service on Monday night and Tuesday night and Thursday night and Friday night." I suddenly found myself hungry for the first time in my life. I had found what I hadn't known before: spiritual truth.

It was then my Pastor became a friend of mine. I looked up to him as he would stand in the pulpit, a six-foot four-inch giant of a man, dying at the age of thirty-eight. I knew he only had a little while to live. I would sit there and think, "Oh God, he is a giant, and he gave to me Your saving Word."

Listen, dear Christian friend, the only way your spiritual life grows is by the Word of God. And that is why you want to study it and be where it is preached and where it is read. That is going to strengthen your spiritual life and make you to grow in Christ.

We are interested in God's children growing, and that is why we teach the Word of God the best we can, and have our teachers teach the Word of God as best they can, because the Word of God is the food of God. Jeremiah said, "Thy words were found and I did eat them and they became as honey and meat and milk to my soul." The Word of God divinely given to us is the Word that delivers life to us, communicates life, and having communicated life to us, it strengthens our life.

THE WORD OF GOD DIRECTS US

Now go to Psalm 73. This is a Psalm where a man looks out upon social injustices, social inequality, and he is angry at life because of what he sees. He is a man of faith, and he just doesn't understand what he sees. He sees the "haves" and the "have-nots" of the world. There are the people who have everything and the folk who don't have anything. He can't understand what is happening. And then he begins to think, and he realizes all that he has in God . In verse 23 He declares, "I am continually with Thee: Thou hast holden me by my right hand. Thou shalt guide me with Thy counsel (that is, with Thy Word), and afterward receive me to glory." So now this Word of God that gives us life and builds up our lives becomes for us a life-directing Word. I need this. I am glad that when the Lord saved me and brought me into His family and gave me His Word, He said, "I have given you my Word to direct your life."

U.S. News and World Report, in a recent issue, carried an article about a new nonprofit organization which plans to popularize the concept that it "pays to do right." In other words, "honesty is the best policy." Where do you suppose they got this idea? And isn't it amazing that we have reached a point in America where people have to be sold on doing right. I read in the newspaper this week that schools in this city have begun teaching morals. Bully for them. May I ask you where did you get your concept of life? *Fortune, Forbes*, the philosophies of men? Do you know that the only place where men find the right principles by which to live is in the Word of God? Do you know that the Word of God teaches honesty and morality? Anything that you would like to be, the Word of God lays down principles by which God would direct your life. I pray that the Lord will allow me to live long enough to spend a year and search the entire Word of God and write down all the principles in the Word as they relate to men. Did you know that in setting down life principles, the Bible doesn't leave out anything? You cannot name an area in your life but what God in His Word has given principles relating to that area. This includes principles for our homes, for families, for husbands and wives, for children, for our jobs and businesses, principles for dealing with the pressures, disappointments and sorrows of life.

We live in a world that has lost its way, lost its standards and its values. The Word of God is of utmost importance in helping us find our way. Men grope to find their own way, and they fail because they do not look to God for truth and direction, the truth and direction found in His Word. God gives us a Word that doesn't change, a Word that is forever settled in heaven and that gives life and strength and direction by which to live.

Father, we ask that someone who has never received this Word, who has never invited the living Word, Jesus Christ, to come in may invite Him today. We thank you for this Word. We pray that it may indeed be our meat and drink and that we may grow in holiness and graciousness and kindness and compassion. May the Word of God be powerful in us we pray. Then help us to pass it on to somebody else, to someone who doesn't know it. Now we pray that there may be a response in our hearts. May we make that response now. Bless us, for Jesus' sake. Amen.